CHRISTIAN
WHOLENESS

THOMAS A. LANGFORD

CHRISTIAN WHOLENESS

NASHVILLE, TENNESSEE

CHRISTIAN
WHOLENESS

Unless otherwise identified, all scripture quotations are from the Revised
Standard Version of the Bible (RSV), copyright 1946, 1952, and © 1971
by the Division of Christian Education, National Council of Churches
of Christ in the United States of America, and are used by permission.

The quotation by Langston Hughes is copyright 1951 by Langston
Hughes. Reprinted from *The Panther and The Lash: Poems of Our
Times,* by Langston Hughes, by permission of Alfred A. Knopf, Inc.

The quotation from "Revelation" is from *The Poetry of Robert Frost*
edited by Edward Connery Lathem. Copyright 1934, © 1969 by Holt,
Rinehart and Winston. Copyright © 1962 by Robert Frost. Reprinted
by permission of Holt, Rinehart and Winston Publishers.

The quotation from the "Choruses from 'The Rock' " is from *Collected
Poems 1906-1962* by T. S. Eliot, copyright, 1936, by Harcourt Brace
Jovanovich, Inc.; copyright © 1963, 1964 by T. S. Eliot. Reprinted by
permission of the publishers.

The quotation by Tom Stoppard is from *Rosencrantz & Guildenstern
Are Dead,* copyright 1967, by Grove Press, Inc. Used by permission of
the publisher.

FIRST PRINTING, January, 1979 (8)
SECOND PRINTING, JANUARY, 1981(8)
Library of Congress Catalog Card Number: 78-58011
ISBN: 0-8358-0383-X
Printed in the United States of America

To

Ann Marie

who embodies what I attempt
to describe

CONTENTS

INTRODUCTION

Christian living is a struggle for wholeness. Wholeness of vision, wholeness of experience, wholeness of relationships, and wholeness of service are all necessary components of Christian maturation.

Seeking wholeness does not mean finding completeness. Maturation is a way of living, not an achievement. It is a process of finding, expressing, waiting, and rediscovering.

God is wholeness, and the possibility of our becoming whole persons is a gift of God's grace. Christian wholeness is set within God's presence to us and our presence in the world.

God's presence in Jesus Christ brings wholeness to human experience. The adventure of the Christian life is found as one lives with the daily struggle of such tensions as self-giving and self-finding, strength and vulnerability, hurt and hope, penance and pardon, excellence and humility, even death and resurrection.

The truth of wholeness is not to be located at a midpoint between these poles; it is to be found by affirming the reality of both poles. Sometimes wholeness is found in reconciling seeming contradictions, sometimes it is recognizing complementarities, sometimes it is holding diversity together even in its diversity. In every case it is a gathering of life, with all its richness and all of its struggle, around a dominant center.

In these meditations we are seeking to depict the texture of life which is represented in full-orbed Christian living. August Bournonville, late leader of the Royal Danish Ballet, has said of ballet what could also be said of Christian living: "Noble simplicity will always be beautiful. The astonishing, on the contrary, soon becomes boring." It is the noble simplicity of Christian living which we seek to explore.

CHAPTER ONE

SELF-GIVING AND SELF-FINDING

Sometimes it is a shock to look at yourself in the mirror. We sometimes look and do not recognize our own faces. We often live with an idealized picture of ourselves. We may have thought that we looked better, more attractive, and more impressive than we now appear. We easily deceive ourselves since no knowledge is more difficult to obtain than self-knowledge. It is more difficult for us to achieve acceptance of ourselves as we are than any other task we must perform.

To accept ourselves we need the acceptance and the affirmation of others. We know this in the unconscious recesses of our lives as well as at the most explicit levels of self-understanding. Because we need the acceptance of others, we spend a great deal of our lives attempting to win that acceptance. We pretend and we put on masks. We present ourselves as we think others want us to be. Time and again we ask, Who do they want me to be? rather than, Who am I? We allow the crowd to set the agenda and to dictate what we will be, do, or say. Desperately wanting to be accepted, we attempt to make ourselves acceptable on other persons' terms.

Our pretensions can be as varied as the persons we are with. We pretend to be better or worse than we are, stronger or weaker than we are, and more intelligent or less intelligent than we are. With chameleon cunning we change color and fit into the context of the moment. But we know that there comes the moment when our camouflage will be removed.

Some years ago a young man I knew on the campus came to talk about his search for identity. Our conversations continued over a semester. As I came to know him better, I became aware of how much he changed as he was in different situations. As he moved from the classroom to the fraternity house to his own home, his posture, his language, his tone, and his way of relating would undergo a metamorphosis; he continually switched one authority for another as he acted the role he thought was expected in each situation.

It is difficult for any of us to accept ourselves, but there are special moments of grace. Grace is present both in the moment when we see ourselves as God sees us and the moment when we know that we have been accepted by God.

God knows and loves us thoroughly. There is no need for acting. God knows who we are and what we are. There is no need for pretension for God accepts us with our weakness and strength, with our evil and our virtue, and with our inability and our ability.

To know that we are loved and accepted by God is the most important knowledge we can gain. It is the primal wisdom. To know that one is pardoned, accepted, and affirmed at the most basic level of life gives the possibility of accepting ourselves and of accepting other persons as they are.

When we know that we have been accepted by God—just as we are—it is possible to accept ourselves as we are and begin to be the person we were created to be. Human life is thwarted in its development into its full potentiality by sin. Sin is always a disordering of our personhood; it is a distortion of life as God has given it and has intended that it should be. On the contrary, salvation is the finding of life as God has intended it to be with the uniqueness which is given to us in our distinctive personhood and our concrete relationships. To know that one is accepted by God is to be able to accept one's self and to begin to be one's self, one's true self.

Self-acceptance which comes from rootedness in relation to God brings with it a freedom to accept others as they are. Other people are no longer a threat. We no longer need to manipulate them or manipulate ourselves in relation to them. We are now able to accept them in terms of their own distinctiveness, even with their contradictory characteristics.

An undergraduate woman confided in me that if a friend was a person with whom one could relax and share intimate things and with whom one could simply be oneself, then she had never had a friend. On the basis of her account, I believed her. For some weeks we discussed friendship, a matter which had become a passionate concern for her. She attempted to find someone to be a friend. She encountered dorm mates and people she met in class, but she was continually frustrated. Her experience brought out a significant truth: We do not establish friendship by attempting to make someone our friend. As desirable as friendship might be, we cannot manipulate persons even for such a good end. Friendship is a gift which comes as we relax with another person and reveal our true selves in the relationship. The need to be related can destroy the very relationship we want to establish.

To put the matter rather sharply: When we no longer need other persons for our own sakes, when we no longer have to demand that they accept us so that we can accept ourselves, when we no longer have to contrive relationships, then we are free for other persons and free to be a neighbor to other people.

How does one find one's self? At this juncture we come to a central theme of Christian self-understanding. Christian faith does two different things at the same time: It draws us out of ourselves, challenging us to radical self-giving, and it reinforces us in ourselves. In giving and receiving there is self-finding.

Christian faith draws us out of ourselves. The good news of God in Jesus Christ is that God has broken into our self-contained world, God has broken into our inordinate self-love and has won our affection. We do not escape ourselves by saying, Here now, I will get out of myself. We are drawn out of ourselves as God evokes our love and becomes the center of our lives. The incarnate love of God in Jesus Christ is the gracious event which brings new life.

Grace constitutes the context and the occasion of our self-giving. Grace is God's initiating love; it is God's incursion into our lostness. Grace is a person; grace is Jesus Christ. As God in Christ draws us into relation with him, we, in response, lose our lives—and find our lives. "For whoever would save his life will lose it, and whoever loses his life for my sake will find it" (Matthew 16:25).

In Jesus we find embodied the self-giving of God to persons and the self-giving of a person to other persons. Jesus is the Lord who is servant, and Jesus is the servant who is Lord. As the Lord who is servant, Jesus identifies with human life so as to establish redemptive relationship. As servant who is Lord, Jesus calls us to acknowledge his lordship through our servanthood. The grace of God in Jesus Christ calls us to a graciousness which is a self-abandonment to the love of God and the love of the neighbor.

Christian faith leads us out of ourselves; it frees us from ourselves as it binds us to God and to our brothers and sisters.

Christian faith also reinforces us in ourselves by offering to us the selfhood which we have not realized. The strange truth of the gospel is that in yielding one's self, one receives his or her personhood. It is through self-loss that one becomes self-possessed. In loving God and our neighbors we radically abandon ourselves; in loving God and our neighbors we are given our true selfhood.

What God demands God gives. This succinct statement fully depicts the gospel of grace. Life is encompassed by God's grace, so self-giving and self-finding take place in God's presence. We love God because God has first loved us (1 John 4:19). We love our neighbor because God in Jesus Christ has been our neighbor and has shown us who our neighbor is and how to be a neighbor.

In giving ourselves we receive ourselves. In Tennyson's words, from *In Memoriam,* such persons

> Rise on stepping-stones
> Of their dead selves to higher things.[1]

The dialectic is clear but it is frightening. We want so desperately to be persons, yet we know how fragile is our hold upon any meaning. We are loath to release what little hope we have. Let go! we are told. But how does one let go of the meager remaining hope? We hold to ourselves as a drowning person holds to a last vestige of support—even when it is obvious that it cannot offer support. We grasp ourselves and sink under our own weight.

When in faith we release our grip and allow ourselves to respond to God's inviting call, we find a buoyancy of grace. We discover that we are able to move and utilize our strength in worship and service.

Our self-image is always a reflected image. We come to know who we are through the relationships in which we live. God in Jesus Christ is the primal reality which creates our primal reality. We are able to explore the full dimensionality of our lives as we increase in our love of God and of our neighbor.

CHAPTER TWO

LIBERATION AND CELEBRATION

Two of the most popular words in present Christian vocabulary are *liberation* and *celebration*. But they are often spoken by conflicting voices and often reflect quite divergent attitudes.

Liberation carries a deep sense of caring. It points toward the transformation of society and calls Christians to action on behalf of the dispossessed, the disenfranchised, and the neglected persons of our world.

Celebration connotes exuberant joy. It is lighthearted. It calls persons to thanksgiving and affirmation. Celebration affirms life and catches persons up into an awareness of goodness, and an exhilaration of positive meaning.

Often these two facets of experience are set in opposition. The advocate of liberation tends to seriousness, empathetically sympathizes with the brokenness of human life and carries the weight of the struggle for emancipation from structures and systems which oppress persons. The celebrant of life tends to affirm meaning already found and expresses that meaning in ecstatic movements of heart, mind, and body. At their worst, those who call for liberation are too intensely serious; and those who call for celebration are frothy and glib. At their best, those who call for liberation know that their contention in this bruised world is a part of God's contention and that God's providence underwrites their efforts. Because of this grace they rejoice. Those who call for celebration know that the good graces of life have been won by God's hard suffering and they, too, encounter debilitating pressures in life.

In Christian wholeness, both liberation and celebration must be held in interactive tension. Each needs the other. Each becomes unbalanced without the other.

The theme of liberation has recently broken upon us with a new urgency. Yet, it has grown from deep spiritual roots—roots which reach through the biblical story. The emancipation of Israel from Egypt, the prophetic denunciation of social immorality, and the ministry of Jesus all point to God's struggle and the struggle of faithful people with the principalities and powers of this world. As Jesus inaugurated his ministry, he brought the prophetic word from the past into his present.

> "The Spirit of the Lord is upon me, because he has anointed me to preach good news to the poor. He has sent me to proclaim release to the captives and recovering of sight to the blind, to set at liberty those who are oppressed" (Luke 4:18; see also Isaiah 61:1).

That word of mission extends from Jesus' time to our own. However, the challenge to participate in the liberation of those who are the wretched of the earth is quickly glossed over. The systems of established power desensitize too many of those who once possessed sensitivity; these systems reward persons into apathy, and they refuse to yield to more tender spirits. Time and again the awareness of the people of God is enlivened only by the excruciatingly bitter cries of those who have been abused. In our own time the voices of those who are denied a place because of race, or sex, or economic depression have been forcing themselves upon our hearing.

There are stellar examples of persons whose responses exhibit liberating service: Mother Teresa in Calcutta, India; Stephen Biko in South Africa; Jesse Jackson in the United States; numerous women in Northern Ireland; and so the list continues. But it continues also among those who receive no publicity and often are put down for their concern: social case workers, organizers of halfway houses, those who work with released prisoners, with unwed mothers, with juveniles in trouble, those who provide transportation for medical services, those who work with mentally retarded children, who care for a sick neighbor, and who shop with persons who need help with the use of money. There are also those who serve liberation causes by working to change systems of financial support, legal rights, and educational opportunity. Again the list goes on, and God alone knows those who are faithful servants in the cause of righteousness.

To be aware of negative, destructive conditions and their cause is a part of Christian sensibility and Christian responsibility. The Christian must always be sensitive to the cry of the abused and must always be willing to participate in their struggle for freedom. The Christian, as heir to the faith of Israel, remembers God's struggle to help exiles and strangers and outcasts. The Christian, as one who has seen God in the face of Jesus Christ, understands that the incarnation was God's identification with the brokenness of our human condition.

The incarnation is crucial at this juncture, for it was the incarnate Lord who carried a cross to the crest of Golgotha and was crucified. And the incarnate Lord meets us in every human need, in every maimed life, and in every hungry, cold, sick, or imprisoned person. "For I was hungry and you gave me food, I was thirsty and you gave me drink, I was a stranger and you welcomed me, I was naked and you clothed me, I was sick and you visited me, I was in prison and you came to me" (Matthew 25:35-36).

A friend told me about a Roman Catholic priest in France, who had been intensely involved in attempting to get an adequate sewage system for his town. He was asked why he worked so hard to provide a sewage system. He answered, "Because I believe in the incarnation." Theologically that is correct; spiritually the answer conveyed a profound sensitivity to God's presence.

Liberation must, for the Christian, begin within the household of faith, but it must extend beyond the church. The community of faith should be in the forefront of those institutions which are attempting to embody a freedom which allows and encourages all people to establish their integrity, to enhance their human potential, and to make their full contribution to others. The church should be a sign for the world that liberation is possible. It should be a community which struggles to embody freedom and wholeness. This need must be spoken to the church as well as through the church.

Within the body of Christ, all artificial boundaries should be broken down and petty alienations should be set aside. The Book of Ephesians fosters this expectation (chapter 2). Even though such liberation is not often found in the actual life of the church, this vision stands as a judgment and as a promise. No Christian can find liberation without working for and affirming the prospect of liberation for every sister and brother. No Christian community can find wholeness without providing every member of the body the opportunity for wholeness. Possessed of promise and mandated for action, the Christian church must bring release and possibility to every person within its orbit.

Liberation also carries a responsibility for our societal context. The church exists for the world, so no Christian community may limit its life to self-enclosing walls. As Christians we are disposed by Christ to serve the world. Every authentic cry for freedom, every hungry stomach, every weak hand, every victim of bigotry stands as a challenge to our determination, and ingenuity, and resources to embody the love of Christ.

The task of liberation is demanding. It requires a

continual awareness of the pains which debilitate human life. It requires hard work, tenacious pursuit, difficult confrontation, and the exercise of courage. Liberation requires sustained sensitivity and effort, political acuteness and practical diligence; it requires vulnerability and strength. Because such effort is so demanding, it can be exhausting. Zeal can turn to vengeance and sympathy can result in exhaustion. Sinclair Lewis commented that the effort to serve people through social causes sometimes turns into using people for the success of the cause. This is always a danger. But there is the reverse danger of allowing the difficulties to drain our desire to attempt to make the systemic changes which are necessary.

Thomas Raymond Kelly, a Quaker mystic, found himself exhausted, spiritually and physically, by his effort to carry what Quakers call "a concern" for all the troubles of the world. He cared so much that he lost his ability to function. Finally, he learned to pray each day for the entire world and then add: "And now, Lord, give me my one special concern for today and show me how to serve that need." He did not stop caring widely and deeply, but he had to learn how to focus his concern and his energy and allow God to exercise the omnipresence of grace for the rest.

The goal of liberation, which so desperately needs to be served, also requires a liberation from its own stringent demands. The effort of liberation requires the counterbalance of celebration.

Celebration is a spontaneous, effulgent moment in the midst of life. It is not a total way of life, but it is a gracious release of the energies of the spirit in loving fellowship with God and in loving community with other persons. Genuine celebration cannot be artificially induced; it is a breakthrough of joy. Celebration wells up from gifts received, presence realized, and promises foreseen. Celebration comes from love shared and love being shared. It moves quickly and thoroughly through the one who is drawn into its ambience.

Celebration as a total way of life is misproportioned. For continuous celebration would be "triumphalistic." It would be surface effervescence. It would be an unconscious insensitivity to the rude negativities of the actual context of life. Celebration can become manic, pretentious, and affected. It can carry blatant expressions of pride and self-serving experience. Celebration may be evidence of spiritual shallowness. But it need not be any of these things. Its authenticity can express an appropriate response to God's gift of fullness of life.

The moment of celebration is a fruit of relationship. It witnesses fulfilled relationship with God and fulfilled relationship with our brothers and sisters. Relationships, when they are good, can produce moments when the other is so thoroughly present that the only possible reaction is spontaneous joy.

The movement of celebration may ripple through any or all parts of the body, the mind, or the emotions. Singing, dancing, embracing, shouting, a quick glance, or the movement of the heart may all express the sense of fulfilled meaning.

The celebrating spirit does not rise by its own power. It responds to the attraction of God. The celebrating spirit is responsive to that releasing grace which throws off all careful calculations of how to relate, of what to ask, of how to act, of what to give. Celebration is ecstatic, that is, it is a standing out from under our normal or conventionally controlled actions and reactions. It expresses love in an overflowing of gratitude.

The essence of the celebrative spirit is thanksgiving. It is an enveloping thanksgiving which is inclusive of all of life. Nature becomes a sacrament to God. Life and its tasks become a receiving and a giving. Our whole selves and our entire context are taken up into this explosive moment.

Music is primitive language, painting is primitive writing, dancing is primitive body speech. It is not surprising that these wellsprings are the media for the expression of celebration, for celebration is a spontaneous expression of the deepest and most pervasive dimensions of life.

Celebration affirms the goodness in life. *Liberation* is aware of the evil in life. Celebration sees life with its positive quality; liberation sees life with its negative repressiveness. Yet each dimension overlaps the other and each needs to interact with the other.

How difficult it is to keep the wholeness! How important it is to keep the wholeness! Liberation and celebration, the world under God and the world in

God are elements of Christian wholeness. They should both be present. Celebration recognizes that liberation is a gracious gift; liberation recognizes what is given. Each complements the other as the Christian lives open to God and open to the world.

"And you are Christ's; and Christ is God's." (1 Cor. 3:23). "You are Christ's"—that is the compulsion for liberation. "And Christ is God's"—that is the compulsion for celebration.

CHAPTER THREE

HURT AND
HOPE

A farmer, who was a friend and a partner in ministry in a small parish I served some years ago, would sometimes say as we talked about situations in the parish, "People are like whip leather; they can stand far more than anyone can imagine." It is amazing what some persons are able to live with, to endure, and sometimes to use creatively. However, before we rush to quick answers and happy settlement, it is necessary to face directly and clearly the hurt which characterizes the lives of many people.

The brokenness of human relationships, the voiding of life caused by persons and circumstances, and the debilitating erosion of meaning are too common to be overlooked or insensitively neglected. Even with the best of intentions we must sometimes be shocked into remembrance of those things we would prefer to forget. Some months ago I walked from a busy morning in my office to the chapel service in the Divinity School. My mind was rethinking the ordinary business of the day, and as the service began I participated in a distant manner. I heard the invocation, sang the hymn, and sat down to listen. Just prior to the congregational prayer, the leader asked if there were special needs which anyone wanted to bring to the group. Spontaneously persons started mentioning events in which they were engaged: a child in a serious accident, a desperately sick man in the hospital, the ravages of a broken home, the separation of a recently married couple. In rapid succession nine persons described need. I was shocked. I had come to worship with a degree of indifference, not especially conscious of any need around me. Yet here I was in a company of concerned people who were at that moment sharing the hurt of the world.

One only needs to be aware of the human community to be overwhelmed by the hurt persons experience. A group of ministers' wives gathered together to talk with an understanding friend. The friend later told me, "I listened the whole time to the hurt they were feeling." A student came to say, "I have been silently screaming for a week, and now I need someone to hear." I listened as a lawyer friend who has no defense against anxiety and self-rejection related his frustration in a moment of release.

The hurt of the world is evident not only in terms of psychological sensitivity. There is a range of physical tragedies which sunder human life: hunger, poor housing, inadequate clothing, inadequate medical care. There is also political tyranny, economic exploitation, injustice, war, racial and sexual bigotry. The list is frighteningly long and may be drawn from the full range of corporate experience. And we feel too inadequate to cope. We shrink from the depiction of these conditions on television or in other news media. We shrink and sometimes attempt to escape and forget rather than involve ourselves in ridding the world of the dark and destructive powers.

Hurt is no respecter of persons. One can walk the streets and see the defeated wino or visit the luxury apartment and see the alcoholic. Abuse of wives, husbands, and children knows no social scale. The harsh agendas of self-love are carried by us all. We live with deformation of body and spirit. We are beggars in rags and velvet. The reality of life presses upon us and we must face the fact of evil, the slicing of pain, the power of destructive forces, the inexplicable accident, the intentional cruelty. How to understand and deal with evil is a central issue for our time, as it has been for every time.

There is no pleasure in recording human hurt. Indeed, it is difficult to relive even so short a set of memories. But there is a necessity to recognize honestly the condition of life. There is a necessity to challenge the continuance of such evil. Hurt is not God's intention for this world. It is a false ordering of life and a perversion of intended meaning. A crucial juncture in life and faith is met when we, who are aware of such hurt, come to know that someone has hurt for us.

The incarnation, as this culminates in the cross, is the ultimate identification of God with persons. God has taken our side in our experience of hurt. God is present with us in our world of brokenness. In our alienation, God is with us. In our inability to reach out and love another person, God is with us. In our distress of mind and emotions, God is with us. God is with us when we are in isolation, in fear, in physical pain, in the midst of organized evil.

God's presence is the ground of our hope. Hope is based not upon our autobiography but upon God's biography. Our hope is in God who has brought and continues to bring healing to our hurt.

The use of the word *world* in the John writings of the New Testament is instructive. The *world* means not only the created order, but it is also a symbol of the powers which are organized against God. It is the symbol of the fallen and hostile creation. In discussing this world and possible relations to it, the John literature seems to take contradictory positions. For example, 1 John 2:15 says, "Do not love the world or the things in the world. If any one loves the world, love for the Father is not in him." Whereas in John 3:16 we have the classical epitomizing of the gospel, "For God so loved the world that he gave his only Son, that whoever believes in him should not perish but have eternal life."

In these two passages the *world* as object remains the same. The distinction lies in the characterization of *love*. Our human love for the world is shallow. We love the world only enough to be transformed by it. God's love for the world is deep—deep enough to transform it.

In God's transformation of life lies our hope. Not everyone believes this. Samuel Beckett, who is disconcertingly perceptive in his analysis of contemporary human existence, has commented that at times of crisis religious faith has about the same depth as an old school tie. In candor we have to say that at times it seems that this is the case. Religion can be shallow, insipid, useful as a cheap salve but lacking in realism, blind to tragedy, and impervious to human hurt.

This may be so, but it need not be so. The resource of Christian faith is God, God who is in Jesus Christ. Here we reach toward true depth. It is God in Christ who moves into the arena of hurting human life, who confronts the evil, the distress, and the lostness of our lives and who brings us hope. Let us pursue the matter by asking, What is hope?

Hope can be cheap. It may be based on a refusal to see things as they really are, or it may be an expression of childish wishing. But hope which is given by the resurrection is hope which has come through the crucifixion. It is hope which has emerged from tragedy, and hope that has looked at evil with clear eyes and has felt actual pain. At the most fundamental level, our hope is in God and as such it is real hope in the midst of real life.

Hope is living in the awareness of God's providence. Hope is a moving forward, a looking toward a final end; but it is also a transformation of the present. Hope is not a reinforcement of simple self-interest; it is not a possession to be hoarded for our own well-being. Hope is God's gift which helps us to live through our hurt and which carries us into the struggle with the hurt of the world. Hope is a sign of

God's presence amidst life's brokenness and makes us present to the world's need.

Christian hope begins with the historical Jesus, remembering his passion and resurrection. Christian hope speaks of Jesus Christ and the future he brings. "All the promises of God find their Yes in him" (2 Corinthians 1:20). Jesus comes as a balm to heal the bruised body of this life, and Jesus goes before us to confront the destroyers of life. As we move to follow, we do so with the confidence which only hope can know.

To be hopeful is to live. To be hopeless is to die.

What happens to a dream deferred?
Does it dry up like a raisin in the sun?[2]

Langston Hughes

But hope, by God's grace, can arise out of the situation of hopelessness. "Exactly where hope ceases to be reasonable it begins to be useful," Soren Kierkegaard said, and in so saying he moves across the barrier where human capability releases itself into God's grace. It is Jesus' resurrection that assures us of God's faithfulness.

God keeps his promises and gives us hope.

In the life, death and resurrection of Jesus
God kept his *promises.*
All that we can ever hope for was present in Christ,
But the work of God in Christ is not over.
God calls us to hope for more than we have yet seen.
In Christ God gives hope for a new heaven and
earth,

Certainty of victory over death,
Assurance of mercy and judgment beyond death.
This hope gives us courage for the present struggle.[3]

Christian hope is practical; it possesses an everyday quality. Christian hope is embodied in our struggles with the concrete conditions of human existence —attacking all limiting, oppressing, demeaning realities. It is in the strength of Christian hope that we are able to endure with the outcast and share the burdens of the weak. Our hope in God informs our life in this world.

Hope refuses to let us be conformed to this world. Leading us far beyond that which has already been accomplished, it shows us the vision of what can be. Living in hope we no longer conform to: our already developed self, our social and economic order, our established culture, our shallow securities, or our self-envisioned goals.

So we return to the *world* in the writings of John. God's love for the world is to be refracted through Christian living. Gracious love goes out even to those who oppose and would negate that love. Here is the world's suffering, but here also is its hope.

In faith and faithfulness we wait upon and participate in the hope which God gives. The hurt of the world which is so pressingly real is not the end. We hope in God—this is the final word.

CHAPTER FOUR

STRENGTH AND VULNERABILITY

Christian strength comes from self-confidence which derives from the confidence we have in God and from the affirmation we receive in Christian community. Vulnerability as a Christian quality comes from our availability to others which is derived from God's constant availability and from our being participants in community with other persons.

Christians need to learn to affirm strength. Too often Christian character is thought of in terms of weakness, self-loss, or anemic living. But to be called and commissioned, to be forgiven and renewed, is to be given personhood and vocational responsibility. To be Christian is to be strong in God, under God, and with God. It is to be strong as persons, for persons, and with persons.

Such self-affirmation is always fraught with the danger of confusing derived strength with self-engendered strength. It is subject to a substitution of personal achievement for gracious endowment. But a reverse temptation must also be recognized, namely a denial of strength, which is actually possessed under the guise of pretended weakness or false humility. The danger of misplaced confidence should not undercut the reality of strength which is actually possessed. False self-assessment from either direction must be overcome by clear and proper self-understanding.

Our strength, as Christians, comes from our relation to God and to the people of God. We are directly related to God, and in that relationship we find our ability to move to action and to live for others. Indirectly we receive the strength of God through sharing in Christian community. This is a sharing which empowers, guides, corrects, and renews our ability to be and to serve.

Emphasis upon Christian strength is often neglected for fear of abuse, and the strength given by community is often neglected because it is so meagerly realized in contemporary experience. Yet the church is the Body of Christ; it is the special embodiment of the Holy Spirit. The church is the community graciously given by God to persons who need and who intensely seek community. Into our solitary, isolated style of living there comes a concrete community of persons who are willing to bear one another's burdens, to enhance one another's living, to be together in joy and in sorrow, in hope and in hurt, at ordinary moments and in critical junctures of human experience.

In the context of the church, strength comes from lives which are bound together. The chief binding is not that of a desperate clinging to one another in a dangerous and frightening world, although there is some truth in the claim that one can endure the stench of the ark only because of the tumultuous waves outside. The deeper truth, however, is that persons in Christian community are bound together by a common love, by a common worship, and by a common mission. The church is the community of persons who are in community with Jesus Christ. It is a community of persons precisely because there is a common center for their lives.

Psychologically it is often the case that we feel our greatest sense of being together when we share a common interest which is beyond us. Several years ago a young friend was talking about her problems with her boy friend. "The only thing we have enjoyed together for the last month," she said, "was washing the car on Saturday." We talked about their difficulties and the reason for the fun at the car wash. Often when we have problems, we concentrate on the problems and let them become the center of our attention. For these two young people, washing the car was the one thing to which they had looked beyond their problems. It was the one thing they had done together in a long time.

In a recent meeting of persons from several ethnic groups, tensions arose and no resolution of the problems being discussed was taking shape. Then one person commented that every time we meet as different races we talk about the problems which exist between us. "Why don't we do something together?" a woman asked. In an effort at common mission, a new sense of unity and commonality was gained. To find a common interest which draws us out of ourselves into common activity can be creative of community.

As a consequence, we are often most together when we do things together, such as listen to music together, or work together, or play together. From a Christian perspective, we are most together as a community when we worship together and when we serve together; that is, when we acknowledge a common Lord and a common responsibility to our Lord.

Strong in God, strong for God—these are basic themes of Christian living. And they are claims which need to be rediscovered. Strength in God points to one of the most basic dimensions of life: To be forgiven, accepted, and affirmed by God is to have a relationship which holds us and which provides a footing upon which our proper self-affirmation can arise. From such a foundation we can move into other relationships and into service of the world. Strength for God is the result of having received strength. Christians cannot be cowards. They must not surrender to hostile challengers. Perhaps the interpretation of meekness as "strength under control" is the best description of Christian strength. Strength as possessed by Christians is strength under the control of the Lord.

To put it plainly, Christian strength is directed by love. It is strength to do good in ways which are compatible with the self-giving of Jesus. Christian strength never implies lording it over others; it never implies that might makes right. It never places self-interest first; it is never used to take advantage of others. Christian strength is strength to serve, to endure, to love, and to give. Perhaps this is the most remarkable strength of all: strength molded by the Holy Spirit into Christlikeness of life. There is a passage in Philippians which puts the matter directly. "Have this mind among yourselves, which you have in Christ Jesus, who, though he was in the form of God, did not count equality with God a thing to be grasped, but emptied himself, taking the form of a servant, being born in the likeness of men" (Philippians 2:5-8).

At this point a word of caution is appropriate. To live a life shaped by the mind of Christ is not a simple imitation of Jesus, an *imitatio Christi*. Such imitation is always counterfeit and often has led to merely outward symbols (such as wearing robes as Jesus did). What is needed is a freedom of spirit and a tenacity of commitment which leads to a Christian innovativeness, an *innovatio Christi,* as Frederick Herzog has helpfully interpreted this responsibility. To be imaginatively innovative as Christians is to live with a keen sensitivity to God's will for us and with a keen sensitivity to our neighbor's need. It is at the intersection of God's love and human need that the Christian must be found and must exercise the strength which he or she possesses.

If Christian life is characterized by strength, it is also characterized by vulnerability. Vulnerability is shaped from two directions: We are vulnerable to the incursion of God; we are vulnerable to the claims of our neighbors.

Vulnerability as Christians begins with our being claimed by God. Our natural posture as prideful people, as people who pretend to control our own lives, always leads to radical self-defensiveness. With adroit thoroughness, we learn to construct walls of defense which attempt to prevent knowledge of ourselves as vulnerable. We learn to pretend that our strength is sufficient, and we are infinitely capable of self-deception, and in more limited ways, capable of deceiving others. Caught in our own self-love, we are unable to break out of the tight cocoon we wrap around ourselves.

There is a psychological principle at work in this self-enclosure. Caring for ourselves issues in an inability to break out of ourselves. We are impotent to break our overweaning self-love, and even our intention to do so by our own strength has a negative consequence. When we, wanting to go to sleep, become conscious of our effort to go to sleep, we only become more widely awake. When we, wanting to forget a tune, become conscious in our effort to forget, we hum what we want to silence. So it is with our efforts to forget ourselves or to escape our inordinate self-love. When we consciously undertake the task, we only reinforce our self-awareness and self-caring. We do not release ourselves. We are released by God's inbreaking claim and by God's wooing in Christ which calls us from ourselves. We become our true selves as we are made vulnerable to God.

Our vulnerability is extended as we become open to the claims of our neighbors. Vulnerability in this dimension may be described as responding care. Vulnerability is sensitivity, feeling the pangs of the hurt of the world, knowing the ache of hunger and nakedness, sensitivity to the lostness and alienation of human existence. But vulnerability also has a positive, responsive quality. It is not infinite reception, rather it is reception in order to react, to move, to answer, to effect a new situation.

To be vulnerable is to learn to receive love as well as to be able to give love. For some persons the ability to accept love which has been offered seems as difficult as expressing love for others. It is a grace to be able to accept love offered as much as it is a grace to be able to offer love to another. There is a special character to this receptivity. Charles Williams in his book *The Descent of the Dove* comments that for many persons it is easier to help others bear their burdens than it is to allow others to help us bear our burdens. As long as we are helping others, we can keep our pride and retain our self-image of importance and place. To allow others to help us bear our burdens is to have to acknowledge need, to become humble, and to recognize the genuine interrelatedness of human life. In this sense, vulnerability means the ability to share life completely.

To be vulnerable means to risk the loss of one's self, to have no self except the self that has cast its lot with the other. So vulnerability leads to identification with the marginal people of our world. Sensitive vulnerableness is a capacity for knowing the vulnerability of others, for knowing the personal and systemic dimensions of depravation, of incapacity, of discrimination, of oppression. To live as a Christian in the world is to live as one who shares the brokenness of the world.

The chief symbol of vulnerability is the cross, for it is the cruciform character of Jesus Christ which becomes our symbol of participation in the throes of the world. In the One who could have saved his life but who chose to give his life, in the One who became incarnate in a world of suffering, in the One who claimed all things for God and for the neighbor, we have the decisive expression of God's character and of God's mandate for Christian disciples.

Such vulnerability affects our thinking as well as our actions. In *Waterbuffalo Theology,* Kosuke Koyama expresses the idea that theological thinking must be pursued with the crucified mind not with the crusading mind. This character of theology means that the person who wants to think about God and about God's world must do so with the qualities which are consonant with God's own way of engaging the world in Jesus Christ.

To be vulnerable is to be open and pliable to God's will; it is to be open and responsive to human need.

Vulnerability and strength always go together. Either without the other is destined to perversion. Each requires the other for its own completion. Strength without vulnerability is tempted to assertive control; vulnerability without strength is tempted to passive acquiescence.

Christian vulnerability has the firm center of Christian strength; Christian strength has the open sensitivity of Christian vulnerability. Vulnerability which counts upon strength and strength which counts upon vulnerability is a dynamic of Christian wholeness.

CHAPTER FIVE

PENANCE AND PARDON

In the year that King Uzziah died I saw the Lord sitting upon a throne, high and lifted up; and his train filled the temple. Above him stood the seraphim; each had six wings: with two he covered his face, and with two he covered his feet, and with two he flew. And one called to another and said: "Holy, holy, holy is the Lord of hosts; the whole earth is full of his glory." And the foundations of the thresholds shook at the voice of him who called, and the house was filled with smoke. And I said: "Woe is me! For I am lost; for I am a man of unclean lips, and I dwell in the midst of a people of unclean lips; for my eyes have seen the King, the Lord of hosts!" Then flew one of the seraphim to me, having in his hand a burning coal which he had taken with tongs from the altar. And he touched my mouth, and said: "Behold, this has touched your lips; your guilt is taken away, and your sin in forgiven." And I heard the voice of the Lord saying, "Whom shall I send, and who will go for us?" Then I said, "Here I am! Send me" (Isaiah 6:1-8).

W e do not carry a heavy sense of sin. When someone speaks about sin, there is a slight nodding of the head but also an indifferent shrug of the shoulders. The reasons for this phenomenon are complex, some good, some bad. To have a proportioned sense of sin can be a sign of healthy mindedness. To have a morbid sense of sin can be unhealthy.

Nathaniel Hawthorne's short story "The Minister's Black Veil" is an example of extremity. A young minister, in the town of Milford, suddenly started appearing with his face shrouded by a black veil. His people were puzzled; the covering indicated penance, but for what? The minister would not say and there was no obvious reason. Was this simply an obsessive sense of sin? Many in the congregation thought so and they may well have been correct. It is healthy to have a view of life which is not oppressive, self-flagellating, troubled by every act, word, or thought. It is good to throw off unnecessary shackles.

But a lack of a sense of sin may reflect a shallowness of experience with God and an insensitivity to others. It may mean that we have not rightly recognized our encounter by the holy, claiming, righteous God; and the poverty of our experience of God results in an inadequate self-appraisal. A deficient awareness of sin may reflect an insensitivity to the welfare of others and of our relation with others. One does not live in this world without directly or indirectly hurting other people. To be insensitive of our complicity or direct action is a sad commentary on the quality of our relationships.

There can be an unwholesome sense of sin; let us admit it. But there can also be a wholesome sense of sin, namely the realization that we stand in a distorted relation to God and to our neighbors.

Part of the greatness of a man like John Bunyan was that he knew the human condition thoroughly and he knew it from the inside. Hence, when he personified malice or pride or gossip or greed, he was enfleshing those qualities which are real in our actual lives. So Bunyan writes of one Mr. Gripe-man, a school-master in Love-gain. "This School-master taught them the art of getting, either by violence, cousenage, flattery, lying, or by putting on a guise of Religion." But such contrivance will be revealed and the culprit be unmasked, for there is a greater sensitivity reflected in recognizing these negative characteristics than in pretending they do not exist.

In our religious sensibility and in our theology we have too often tended to interpret God as pliably loving, as lacking distinctiveness of character, as passively tolerant, and as such allowing us to be what we want to be and do what we choose to do. We have generally lost the sense of God's holiness and God's demand for holiness. God is love; that is a basic truth. But that truth has consequences, for love not only defines evil as its contrary, love judges evil, and love finally overcomes evil. Such is holy love. It prevails by the power—the suffering power —of God.

Too often we have tended to excuse or explain away the personal and the systemic evil which we represent and which we, with native quickness, express in our actions. How pervasive evil is; its roots run deep, deep into the soil of our lives and our communities. We live truncated and debilitated lives. Our humanity is a pale imitation of its authentic promise. We live estranged from other people, alienated from God, separated from our own true selfhood. We must once again come to recognize those very real and vital negative dimensions of our lives and our duplicity about those dimensions.

Penance is being honest; it involves looking at ourselves straightforwardly. It is taking ourselves seriously but God more so. Penance is a candid recognition of our person, our place, and our purpose. A proper view of God's righteousness brings a proper view of ourselves. How petty is our pride when we stand in God's presence, how small our achievement, and how inconsequential our moral development. Yet such an honest view of ourselves is difficult to achieve.

In the Apocryphal book of *Ecclesiasticus* the insightful writer says, "A man's soul is sometime won't to bring him tidings, More than seven watchmen that sit on high on a watch-tower" (37:14 REVISED VERSION). Listen to some of the tidings of the soul, be attentive enough to hear some of the messages of the spirit!

It is natural for us to pretend—to pretend that we are strong and able and good and pious. It is even natural for us to attempt to deceive ourselves. We overstate our ability and our achievement. We are hypocritical about our virtue and pretentious about our spirituality. We move through life like an armored knight, exalting in our appearance, issuing challenges, thinking of ourselves as superior, as persons of high quality. The watchmen in the tower announce our coming with appropriate intonations of admiration. Yet the rustle of a dry leaf under the horses' hoofs causes a shiver to run down our spine. Our soul has brought its own tidings; our pretense is shallow and weak, beneath the splendid armor there is a frightful insecurity.

Henry VI, Shakespeare's naively wise king, speaks:

"And he but naked, though lock'd up in steel,
Whose conscience with injustice is corrupted." [4]

Traditionally, penance has been composed of four aspects: contrition, confession, satisfaction, and absolution.

Contrition is the recognition that we as unholy, unworthy people are living in the presence of the holy, loving God. Consequently, we *confess* by specifying those things which have won our hearts from God and torn our love from others.

Then, and it follows of necessity, we must attempt to make *satisfaction,* in so far as we are able, for the things which we have spoiled, the relationships we have broken, and the wrong we have done. As the climax, there is *absolution,* the forgiveness of God.

All of these elements remain important. Although in Protestant worship, absolution, as a sacrament, has been replaced by words of pardon and assurance; that is, by a restating of God's gracious forgiveness.

Perhaps we can draw these themes together. Penitence takes place in the context of grace. In the act of penance all our defenses are dropped, all our pretensions are set aside. We acknowledge we are fallen. We offer our lives to God. As penitents we attempt to amend the wrongs we have done as those who are forgiven and renewed.

Repentance possesses a strange inner tension. It is an act we fear yet one which we want to do. We are, at one level, reluctant to be found out, to be known as we are. So we duck and hide and put on the expected, protected face. But at another level, we want to be known as we are; we seek the freedom which comes from lack of pretension. Perhaps Robert Frost knew this. He writes,

> We make ourselves a place apart
>   Behind light words that tease and flout,
> But oh, the agitated heart,
>   Till someone find us really out.[5]

There is great release in being found out by the love of God and in being able to relax into relationship with God. To repent is to recognize God as the center of life. Douglas Steere once commented that a saint is one who has determined from among all things the one thing he or she loves most and that one thing is God. Penance brings about this refocusing of life. For the narrow way is the focused way, it is life focused upon God.

To repent is to forsake our extravagant self-center-
edness and to place God and our neighbor at the
center of our interest and action. There is no such
thing as separating our sins against God and our sins
against our neighbors. To sin against our neighbor is
sin because it is a violation of the intention of God
who has created us to love our neighbor with a full
heart and mind and strength. To sin against our
neighbor is to be unfaithful to the act of God in
Christ who has shown us what unselfish neighbor
love should be. The good life is a richly giving life; it
is life extended to the neighbor.

Penance is an act before God, and as such, it is an
act of love in response to love. Penance is an act of
hope in anticipation of grace.

Our confession of sin is within the context of
grace. We could not confess if there were no grace.
In truth, of course, our penance begins because we
already know that forgiveness exists. One does not
put down one's armor in the face of evil; one does
not drop his or her weapons—fragile as they may be
—when meeting destructive evil. Penance which does
not know that it is a confession of violation of love
is uninstructed. Penance which does not expect the
renewal of life is pointless.

We can honestly reveal ourselves before God because God cares for us more than we care for ourselves. We can expose our weakness because we can
count on God's strength. We can accept ourselves as
sinners because we already know God's forgiveness.
And this is why penance, in our worship, is connected

with words of assurance. We can be serious about ourselves because we can relax about ourselves.

Hence penance culminates in pardon and in the assurance that we can be whatever—and everything —God wants us to be. Words of pardon bring life into its proper context. They provide a clear recognition of ourselves before God in whom "we live and move and have our being" (Acts 17:28).

To receive pardon, expressed in words of assurance, is to experience a new freedom for life. We often attempt to carry too much; we undertake too many things. We take our importance too seriously; we pretend too much knowledge, too much virtue, too much spirituality. And we have a desperate sense of trying to hold our lives together. To repent is to release our hold upon ourselves. Words of assurance remind us of God's hold upon us. "Peace I leave with you" (John 14:27). "My grace is sufficient for you" (2 Corinthians 12:9).

Some years ago an undergraduate walked silently into my office. He sat for over five minutes before he could speak. Then in a broken voice he said, "I can't do everything I am supposed to do." That was all he was able to say. This young man, who had always been responsible, knew that his strength was at an end. He knew the negative side of his efforts, but he had not yet found any positive possibility. It is here that words of assurance must be uttered. "Cast all your anxieties on him, for he cares about you" (1 Peter 5:7). And it is only here—with God— that new possibility is born.

Pardon, which principally means to release, to cancel, to excuse, or to forgive, must, from a Christian perspective, also possess positive truth. Pardon is a positive activity; it is a mode of dealing with the past in order to enhance the future. Pardon reflects a renewed relationship and carries the promise of growth. Pardon is a cleansing which is, at the same time, a filling. Penance without pardon is incomplete. If one cleanses the house and simply leaves it, seven devils worse than the first can enter and occupy its place (Matthew 12:45).

In worship, pardon is closely tied to words of assurance. This assurance is based upon God's activity which forgives, accepts, and creates new life. We have returned to our point of beginning. Isaiah saw the Lord, he saw himself and he cried, "Woe is me." But he also experienced a cleansing. "Then flew one of the seraphim to me, having in his hand a burning coal which he had taken with tongs from the altar. And he touched my mouth, and said: 'Behold, this has touched your lips; your guilt is taken away, and your sin forgiven' " (Isaiah 6:6-7).

There it is: an act of forgiveness and words of assurance. "And I heard the voice of the Lord saying, 'Whom shall I send, and who will go for us?' Then I said, 'Here I am! Send me' " (Isaiah 6:8).

Isaiah's vision is complete. A vision of God. A vision of the self in contrition before God. A vision of the self raised by God. A vision of the self in the service of God and the neighbor.

Read, then, a prayer of confession and some words of assurance.

O almighty God, give us grace to approach thee at this time with penitent and believing hearts. We confess that we have sinned against thee and are not worthy to be called thy children; yet do thou in mercy keep us as thine own. Grant us true repentance, and forgive us all our sins: through Jesus Christ our Lord. Amen.[6]

"Come now, let us reason together," says the Lord: "though your sins are like scarlet, they shall be as white as snow; though they are red like crimson, they shall become like wool" (Isaiah 1:18).

For God so loved the world that he gave his only begotten Son, that whoever believes in him should not perish but have eternal life. (John 3:16).

Amen.

CHAPTER SIX

LOVE AND
JUSTICE

In Christian devotion there is no word more easily spoken, no claim more immediately responded to, and no notion more difficult to apply than *love*. In social responsibility there is no word more often uttered, no theme more generally affirmed, and no notion more difficult to apply than *justice*. Hence, in Christian ethical theory, there is a constant necessity to understand and utilize the meaning of *love* and *justice,* each in its own right and both in mutual relation.

First there is *love*. God is love, but love is not God. God always remains a mystery; no language can completely capture the depth of divine reality. No human conduct can capture the fullness of God's richness. No combination of concepts and deeds can fathom or express the depths of God. Yet as one attempts to depict the meaning of God in Jesus Christ, one can only say with the writer of 1 John, "God is love" (4:8). Love is the most complete and explicit depiction of God which human beings can frame.

And love is the most thorough and concrete expression of Christian discipleship. So the Gospel of John has Jesus instruct his followers: "A new commandment I give to you, that you love one another; even as I have loved you, that you also love one another'' (John 13:34). To walk in the way of Christ is to walk the way of love.

God's love and the response of human love form the fundamental dialectic of Christian being and they set in motion the possibility of Christian doing. But now, in the most practical terms, what does it mean to express love? Toward God, love is expressed as worship; toward the neighbor, love is expressed in radical self-giving and in creative building of human community.

When we use the word *love* in relation to other persons, we often mean a quality of relationship. We mean the value we place upon others and the way in which we nurture that value. Several words help to capture important aspects of the quality we seek and serve.

Sensitivity: A sensitive openness to others which wants to hear the other speak of himself or herself is fundamental in this relationship. In sensitive relation one encourages the other to express their integrity and to live with that integrity. Sensitivity allows us to hear the other's cry, to share pain, to reach out and join in common joy.

Forgiveness: Forgiveness is a positive not a negative attitude and activity. To forgive is not simply to forget, rather it is the establishment of a good relation over against negativities which might have broken the relationship. To forgive is to remember negatively without negativity. To understand the meaning of forgiveness, we can turn this Anglo-Saxon word around: to forgive is to *give* oneself *for* the other in renewal of community. This is simply a strengthened form of the verb *to give* or *grant*. It emphasizes the unconditional nature of the act which it represents.

Loving forgiveness seeks completeness. It is not a burying of the hatchet but leaving the handle exposed. Forgiveness crosses over to the other. It is a crossing, a cross, which establishes a positive relationship of new possibility and growth.

Claim: To have the quality of relationship which love demands is to challenge the other in honest and supportive ways to be the person he or she was created to be. It is to call persons to release themselves into relationship and into mutual sharing of life. To fail to call persons into account with God and themselves is to fail in love. This claim is not a condition of relationship, but it is an expectation of relationship. Love asks of the other what the other is capable of being and doing.

Community: From a Christian perspective, human relations reach toward full realization when there is a common love, when there is shared faith in God and joint commitment to God. To love God together with others is to be drawn into the deepest sharing of life with one another. It is to find the true base of community and it is to extend community. A new dimension of relationship is established by common life as each person is drawn out of his or her subjectivity into a new way of being as "we" is created.

Love is the bearer of this new way of being, and this new way of being is the inclusive expression of Christian love.

The character of Christian love is depicted most graphically in the parable of the Good Samaritan (Luke 10:30-37). Soren Kierkegaard has indicated an important aspect of this story. The setting of the parable is found in a question. Jesus has emphasized neighbor responsibility and now he is asked, "Who is my neighbor? For whom am I responsible?" In response Jesus tells the story of a man who was robbed and beaten as he was going from Jerusalem to Jericho. A priest and a Levite passed him by, but a Samaritan stopped to help. The Samaritan attempted to aid the stranger, then took him to an inn and paid the innkeeper to take care of the wounded traveler. When he had told the story, Jesus asked, "Which of these three, do you think, proved neighbor to the man who fell among the robbers?" Jesus turned the issue around. The people had asked, "Who should we help? Who is our neighbor?" Jesus asked in return, "Are you a neighbor?" In effect he told them to quit attempting to calculate who the neighbor is, who is worthy of concern, who needs help most. Rather they are to be responsible for their own action. When one is a neighbor, then every person he or she meets, the first one and every one, is a neighbor. Because we are the neighbor, everyone is our neighbor.

In New Testament terms we are talking about *agape. Agape* does not, as do the other Greek words for love, *philia* and *eros,* ask about the quality of the other. Is the other person a peer? Is he or she superior? What is the nature or condition of the other? *Agape* is spontaneous in its expression of concern; and, because it asks no questions, it is universal in its reach. Yet the neighbor is also specific. He or she is the next person and every person we meet. *Agape* says more about the character of the person who extends love than it does about the person who is the recipient of love.

Henri Beyle Stendahl in his novel *The Red and the Black* (in an entirely different context) has expressed this characteristic of love when he comments, "Love does not seek out its equal, love creates its equal." It is this outgoing concern for the other which is the most distinctive mode of Christian love, and it is distinctive in that the responsibility of the one who expresses love is given primacy.

Now we move to the other side. We turn from love to justice, or, more exactly, we turn in love to justice. Justice is one of the qualities which expresses love. Both justice and love have their own integrity. Each has a comprehensive range of meaning; each signifies a way of dealing with persons and with social structures.

Love as the creator of community and as the sustainer of community must seek the well-being of everyone, including the dimensions of social justice. It must seek the well-being of each one within the social group. Love must be joined to public power, Reinhold Niebuhr has argued, if it is not to be impotent in the world. So justice becomes a strong instrument of love as love comes to expression in social situations. Justice has its rootage in those concrete institutions that prescribe duties and protections so that shared goals may be realized.

On the negative side, sin must also be viewed in terms of its social character and its social implications. Sin is not simply personal and is not simply a violation of one-to-one relations. Sin also has a systemic character expressed in structural arrangements. Walter Rauschenbusch used to speak of the "superpersonal forces of evil," and Paul Tillich has spoken of the "demonic" element in organized human life. In the arena of social life, love contends with the negative powers, and sometimes this contention is the contention for justice. Love always demands justice as a primary expression in corporate life.

At the height of the civil rights movement of the sixties, I heard Martin Luther King, Jr. speak. It was a powerful experience when he said, "I don't care whether or not you love me, just give me justice." He was putting theological principle in a starkly practical setting. Love is often falsely interpreted solely in terms of personal relationships. Thus, while advocating love, many persons were not providing the elemental forms of justice for blacks in American society. However, love which denies justice is denying itself.

While love is not identical with justice, it can never allow less than justice. When we allow these qualities to be separated, for instance when charity is promoted and justice neglected, we tend to care for those who are crucified and remain loyal to the institution which does the crucifying.

A number of temptations face the person or the group which is seeking a social expression of Christian love. In a pluralistic society there is a tendency to believe that right and wrong are simply matters of custom or convention which vary with time and place. The result is a disturbing decay of conscience which justifies everything which is not illegal. There are persons who always do what they want to do and always have pious reasons for doing it.

The chief danger for religion in a pluralistic age where everything is tolerated is that it sanctions the existing situation, and this usually means giving society as hostage to the most powerful. Might then does make right. A religion which began as a revolutionary challenge can forget its mandate to establish real justice. But love demands precisely this critical opposition. Oscar Wilde commented caustically that there are people who "know the price of everything and the value of nothing," and that for many "Religion is a fashionable substitute for faith." So it might be that so-called personal piety can be a substitute for the seeking of justice, such as when one seeks his or her well-being in personal isolation rather than in the public arena.

The demand for both love and justice is based upon the confidence that God in Christ is at work in history. Revelation and revolution are closely intertwined. The inbreaking of God's Kingdom into human history radically changes standard values and entrenched human norms. Love and justice become revolutionary expressions of God's historical presence.

The claim of love and justice in Christian community is greater than upon the political community. The church is the immediate arena of the operations of Christian discipleship. Therefore the church must always struggle to be that community which realizes the full range of meaningful life together. The church exists in actualizing love, justice, loyalty, and truthfulness in its own life and extending these into more comprehensive political structures.

Alfred North Whitehead has reminded us that, "The worship of God is not a rule of safety—it is an adventure of the spirit." [7] To worship God truly is to find the confluence of love and justice. The Old Testament, especially the prophetic tradition, makes the two inseparable. The New Testament continues this emphasis, and modern disciples who struggle to hold the two together discover new meaning in Christian wholeness.

CHAPTER SEVEN

COMMITMENT AND OPENNESS

One of the most usual oppositions in popular Christian understanding is that between *commitment* and *openness*. If a person is committed, so the interpretation goes, he or she cannot be open to other perspectives, to other options, or to a change of position. If a person is open, there is implied a refusal to make a commitment; a holding in abeyance all firm convictions and persuasions.

In practical terms this means that one cannot be committed in faith and, at the same time, honest in dealing with contrary evidence. One cannot be committed in faith and be fair or generous to persons of other faith commitments. One cannot be committed in faith and possess empathy for those with whom he or she differs. Many persons take these consequences to be necessary. If it is the case, then we have, by our commitment, set aside some of the most valuable qualities in human experience. But is it so? And even if this is the case for many persons, should it be so? Is it possible for a Christian to be both committed and open?

To be a Christian is to be committed to the lordship of Jesus Christ. This is obvious, but it merits restatement in our day. In a time when there is so much self-interested affirmation, psychological manipulation, and fanaticism among "true believers," there is a tendency to play down commitment. Afraid of excesses and uneasy about authoritarian repressiveness, there has been a tendency to look askance at commitment.

Yet we have commitments, for to be a person is to have a nucleus of values around which life is grouped. To be a part of a community is to share some values with others in the community. If these commitments are not out in the open and clear, if they are not overt, then they will be covert and function in unacknowledged ways. Covert commitments, which are sometimes hidden from ourselves as well as others, are potentially more pernicious than overt commitment; for when commitment is unacknowledged it can neither be critically examined nor intentionally served.

So we put ourselves on the line. To be a Christian is to be committed to Jesus as Lord. And this commitment points to a distinctive way of being; it points to concrete decisions, perspectives, and styles of living. Christian faith is not to be understood as a vague sense of "believing" or a generalized, warm emotion which is invoked by certain rituals, words, or objects. To be Christian is to have committed oneself to the lordship of Jesus Christ. This commitment, whether expressed in one or in a series of moments, becomes the definitive context in which life is lived.

But let us look at the dynamics of commitment.

Too often we hear of destructive oppositions: If you have faith, you cannot doubt; if you are committed, you cannot be open to other perspectives. We have lived with absolute and exclusive notions of faith and commitment. We have known the destruction of fanaticism and the vindictiveness of narrow loyalty.

Christian commitment develops in many ways. For some it occurs in a quick and radical intellectual conversion. For others it is a spontaneous awareness that one believes with the heart what the head has long known. For others it is a slowly developing, at times unconscious, sense of the meaningfulness of life under the lordship of Jesus. And for still others it has to do chiefly with moral rectitude, with sensitivity to the condition of others, or with an appreciation of new moral values. Experiences may extend indefinitely. Commitment may take as many forms as the persons who become committed.

The dynamics of commitment for many people may best be described in terms of the ways in which human relationships are begun. Let us use the analogy of courtship and marriage as a primary illustration. Relationships often begin with an awareness of something which is attractive about another person. It may be physical appearance, the values the other person holds, or an interest in the things the other person enjoys. Almost any quality, if it elicits attention, can attract one person to another.

After this initial attraction there is a time, of varying length, in which these common possibilities are explored. This is courtship. First, casual dating or being with one another, then more serious discussions, more intense involvements, and more extended time together. Throughout this period one is, either consciously or unconsciously, asking whether the qualities which initiated the interest are deep enough or rich enough or extensive enough to hold their lives together. And at any point the answer may be no.

If the relationship develops positively, there is further exploration of the ways in which life can be shared; there are times of shared pleasure and joy and times of shared pain and concern. If, through all of this, there is an increased sense of the value of being together, the courtship may issue in engagement. Now the persons involved make plans to be married. Even after the engagement there may be questions, for it is common in life that the most basic decisions are the most difficult to make. There is seldom absolute assurance where decisions which involve persons at the most personal dimensions of their lives are concerned. This is true of vocational decisions, of responsible personal commitment, and of faith affirmations. As a university teacher, I have had a number of young people come by after their engagement and before their marriage to say that they are not absolutely sure that they should get married. This is typical and while it is a sign for further assessment, in itself it is not necessarily a sign that the relationship is wrong.

At marriage a thorough commitment is made. This level of commitment is fundamental and is intended to endure. Commitment becomes faithfulness, steadfast loyalty, enduring love. No other relationship between human beings is more important; no other commitment to another person more thoroughly affects all of our other decisions. Yet even within marriage there are times of doubt, struggles to renew, and experiences of growth. It is a strange but true phenomenon that years after one has been married there is an awareness that the reasons for affirming the marriage are different from those which originally persuaded one to marry. One has come to value new things in the other person, or one has seen development of some values which were formerly only insipiently present, or, as is often the case, both persons have grown into new values which are jointly shared. Marriage vows are intended to be final, and one should enter into marriage only if this is the intention. But even here—perhaps especially here— one must remain open. And now the openness has subtly but significantly changed, for now the openness is not a consideration of alternative possibilities (requiring a continuous courtship predicated upon uncertainty of commitment). This is an openness to the new possibilities of the relationship; one is open to the fathomless reality of the other person.

So much for the illustration, now for the point. Religious commitment has much this same character. Commitment to God begins with a sense of the importance of the One who solicits faith and discipleship. There is a sharing of life, initially in tentative, exploratory ways. When this proves positive, there is further exploration. It is significant in the Synoptic Gospels' account of the ministry of Jesus that Jesus had spent the major part of his ministry with his disciples before he asked them who they thought he was (Mark 8 and Matthew 16). It was only after they had shared life with Jesus that the early disciples were in a position to make a judgment as to who he was. But in the process of sharing life, of being together, there comes a time when a person must declare his or her intentions and a firm commitment must be made. In Christian discipleship, one speaks those faithful words, "Jesus is Lord." Now every other relationship, every other decision, and every other activity is drawn into the orbit of this commitment.

A word of caution is needed. While we have used human relationships to illustrate personal relationship with God, the analogy is not exact. There are some basic differences. The relationship with God is not one of equals as it is with persons. God is sovereign and we are God's creatures. Yet, we dare to talk of relationship because of God's intention to establish a covenant with persons. This intention is the major theme of the Old Testament and of the incarnation where God enters into our condition and calls us into faithful community. In the divine-human encounter, God is always the initiator. It is the operation of grace which creates the possibility and encourages the actuality of relationship. Once more, the religious commitment is the most primary commitment possible for human life; nothing else, even our most intimate human relationships, can take that foundational position. Finally, God is always faithful. God's steadfast love remains constant. All of these factors qualify our illustration. The relationship with God has distinct qualities, but to enter into a committed relationship has its closest analogies with human relationships.

Yet the question persists. Is it really possible for a person to be committed and yet remain open. Can a person be committed and at the same time . . . open to other options, to new truth, to persons with other commitments, and to new possibilities in relationship?

To be committed is first of all and most important of all to be committed in a relationship, to be committed to God in Christ as a person. Our commitment is not at the most basic level a commitment to propositional expressions of this relationship or to explicit moral imperatives traditionally drawn from this relationship. Our commitment is a response of love with all of the strength and vulnerability of love. To be committed is to be faithful in our relationship with Jesus Christ. We are held and should hold fast to Jesus Christ, but to everything else we should sit loose.

Now we must comment on our relationship with God, and our participation in the new covenant. In every relationship we must be completely honest. Pretense is of little value. If there is doubt, then doubt should be acknowledged. If there is faith, faith should be affirmed. We do not need to pretend. We can bring our entire life before God and into relationship with God. We can be open because we are already open before God.

Openness is such a vague, inexplicit notion. What does it mean in this context? Several meanings of this term are important for our consideration. To be open is to refuse to identify our own knowledge with the truth of God. Even in our understanding of God we are limited by our humanness, for God is beyond our comprehension. The fullness of God is beyond the compass of any words we can use in description. To let God be God, to be aware of our need to know more than we already know, and to learn what we have not learned are parts of being open.

Openness also means not allowing relationships to become static. Good relationship always provides new possibility for further sharing and fresh possibility for common experience.

To be open means that every decision we make as persons must be reaffirmed as we enter into new contexts of life and encounter new temptations.

To be open is to oppose imperialism and manipulation of others. It is the willingness to be related to persons with a patient, hopeful, caring grace which characterizes God's relation to us in Jesus Christ. This willingness prepares us to learn more about Jesus Christ from others, a rich diversity of others. We are willing to see beauty created by or indicated by others, a rich diversity of others. We are willing to acknowledge goodness where it appears' in the lives of others, a rich diversity of others.

Commitment in love is always determined in its character by the love revealed in Jesus Christ. This commitment is affirmative, positive, and constructive. It is as firm and faithful and caring as God's commitment on the cross and in the resurrection of Jesus.

The most difficult question, however, is this: Can one who has made a commitment really be open to a denial of that commitment? In truth we have to say that one may be unfaithful, that one may deny even the most basic commitment. But this is not to say that one simply remains open to alternative possibilities and that the exercise of such openness is a natural response. Commitments have consequences. To make a commitment is to accept its consequences. Openness is liberty in the bond of community. If there is unfaithfulness, as there often is, this is not to be excused by reference to openness. Unfaithfulness is to be acknowledged as wrong. Unfaithfulness is not to be excused, but it may be forgiven. Commitment to God is underwritten by the grace of God.

The firm center of commitment provides the freedom of openness. Together they contribute to Christian wholeness.

CHAPTER EIGHT

JUSTIFICATION AND SANCTIFICATION

Some old and honored words become archaic and are difficult to infuse with new life. One recognizes their prominence and renders appropriate respect, but little hope is held for any understanding of the role these old words can play in the present. *Justification* and *sanctification* are such words.

The doctrine of justification by faith *(sola fide)* or, to be theologically more correct, justification by grace through faith, holds a unique place in the Protestant Reformation. E. C. Hoskyns and F. N. Davey capture the historical significance of this concept: "It was one of those classical moments of intense theological perception, when one Word, one Dogma, one cry of repentance, one assurance of reconciliation appear to contain in themselves the whole truth of God and the whole duty of man." [8]

Justification has an honored place in Christian history, but it has fallen on hard times. The doctrine is remembered but too rarely utilized. Paul Tillich, after making numerous attempts to talk on this theme, concluded that it was such a strange notion to contemporary people that there was scarcely any way of making it intelligible.

Sometimes revered themes become overburdened

by idolization and conflict, by confusion and redefinition, by overfamiliarity of expression and strangeness of setting. Justification by grace through faith is the entrance into Christian life and must be freshly reclaimed by every generation. Justification is God's activity and an expression of God's gracious intention for persons. Justification draws human life into a participatory relationship with God by faith.

The source and power of justification is from God. Yet the motive and mode of God's justifying is beyond human capacity to fathom. It is the mystery and miracle which Bernard of Clairvaux called the "device of ineffable love." The achievement of God's justification changes the status of human life and becomes the foundation of new being in Christ. Justification by grace through faith sets the alternative to forms of self-justification. Justification is not the goal of moral or spiritual effort or the final attainment of a lifetime of obedience and struggle. It is, rather, the presupposition of Christian life and the foundation of Christian experience.

Use of the word *faith* indicates that justification is not a human achievement. Faith recognizes that it is an act of God in Christ and not our experience, our feelings, or our sensitivity which is crucial. Nevertheless, justification reaches from God to persons and solicits and includes our response.

Justification is God's act of setting right, of providing new life for those who have lost the meaning of life. It is an expression of love for the ungodly, an act of renewal for the dispirited, a forgiveness for those who have violated relationship with God and neighbors.

To reclaim the meaning of justification by grace through faith requires a new portraying of the crucified Christ, by word and sacrament, and a fresh recognition of human life as despoiled and then renewed in the context of that grace. The first move toward such reclamation is to keep constantly and clearly before us the unlimited generosity of God.

One effort at restating the meaning of justification by grace through faith is Paul Tillich's emphasis upon accepting the fact that we have already been accepted by God.

Nothing seems more difficult for the sensitive conscience than self-acceptance. We seek admiration by flexing our muscles or showing our intelligence. We seek sympathy by carefully exposing our weaknesses. We are infinitely clever in our search for acceptance; and most insidiously, we presumptuously pretend to spiritual depth and moral righteousness. Yet every pretension attempts to hide deep-rooted self-uncertainty. Inordinate pride is an expression of deception, deception of ourselves and deception of others, while in the crevices of our lives there remains a profound self-doubt and an inability to relax and accept ourselves. As Kierkegaard has said, we know the midnight hour will come when we must remove our masks.

Justification, or acceptance by God, comes to us as we are. We do not need to pretend, we cannot hide, we are thoroughly known and thoroughly accepted by God. In our weakness and in our strength, with our intellectual pride and our moral posturing, we are accepted. "While we were yet sinners Christ died for us" (Romans 5:8).

One of the most perceptive television programs, from a theological point of view, was "The Twilight Zone." I remember one episode about a man who is fully confident of his ability to control his life; all that is required is cool rationality. The man is in an accident and is paralyzed, but he is conscious and rational. Even though the ambulance drivers mistake him for dead, he is convinced that the opportunity will come when he can make his real condition known; so he patiently and thoroughly assesses the situation. He is taken to the hospital and placed on a rolling bed. By this time he has found that one of his fingers is not paralyzed. With confidence he begins to tap the finger on the metal frame of the bed, but the click of the casters is in time with his tapping and drowns out his signal. Finally, he realizes that he is at the end of his capacity. As the attendants push him into the morgue, one of them takes a last look and cries, "There's a tear in his eye. He is alive." It is at the point of our recognition of our need for God, the point of the tear in our eye, that grace brings renewing power.

Another way of speaking about justification by grace through faith is to recognize that in our ordinary, self-sufficient, everyday way of living, we are estranged from God and, consequently, we live with a lack in our humanity. We live with an inadequate

73

development of our human selfhood. In short, we have lost the image of our creation.

Justification is God's reestablishment of the possibility of our true humanity, his restoration of human life to its original intention. Gracious love has given us the possibility of living in the relationships for which we were created and only in which we can find our true humanity.

To be Christian does not make us more than human. It does not make us angelic. It allows us to become the persons God created us to be. Not to have God, the true God, at the center of our lives is to fail to actualize the full dimensionality of our human potential.

There is a basic sense in which we do not understand sin except in the light of grace. We do not understand the negativity of broken relationships except in the presence of whole relationships. We do not understand unloving life except in the experience of love. So the meaning of justification, both in terms of what is overcome and what is gained, is only understood in confronting the act of justification. We know why we were unacceptable in the process of learning that we are accepted. We know the meaning of our creation only in the event of gracious reoffering of our created and creative potential.

Such justification is significant for God and for persons. It is an expression of God's character, an expression which is won only through suffering. It is an event of human redemption, an event which sets us in a new relationship, calls forth a new self-understanding, and sets us to new styles of living.

Now we reach a turning point, for justification is only a beginning. By this grace we enter the Christian life, but life as growth and justification must extend into sanctification. In Christian liturgy baptism is especially the sacrament of justification and the eucharist (the Lord's Supper) is the sacrament of sanctification. Hence baptism occurs once and the eucharistic meal is an ongoing means of grace.

Sanctification, however, is also a strange, archaic word and its meaning needs to be reclaimed. The overtones of this word seem to take us back to a world that has now passed. It seems at least a century out of date, doesn't it? It should not, for the Christian doctrine of sanctification has to do with growth and maturity. It involves the passages of life, and the continuous finding of our human personhood. None of these is out of date even if we only occasionally grasp its significance.

Sanctification is a sign of maturation in Christian living. Every person is to some degree mature, for to be a person means that there has been growth, there has been some integration and shaping of life, and there has been some achievement of self-identification. But even while we may all claim some maturity, we must also be in the process of becoming more mature. Every level of growth provides new possibility for further growth. Every discovery of meaning makes possible new discovery of meaning.

Some years ago I heard E. Stanley Jones say, "To

be most Christian is to be most natural." At the time
I thought he was simply wrong. His comment ran
against what I thought was a theologically valid
interpretation of fallen human nature. But I have
come to believe that he was profoundly right. To be
most Christian is to be in the process of realizing the
humanity which God intends for us. To be Christian
is to live with the community of God and other
persons. It is to be answering the call of our creation, and it is to be responding to the goal of our
lives.

The richness in our diversity as persons is amazing
in its breadth. Because of this diversity, our growth
as persons takes a number of different routes. Sometimes our development is slow and persistent; sometimes it becomes distorted or is annulled. Sometimes
our growth is quick, sometimes ungainly. Sometimes
new growth must be cultivated; sometimes it is spontaneous. Sometimes the changes which take place
seem to produce obvious value; sometimes they seem
to leave more behind than has been gained.

But in all of its diversity, growth as maturation is
always a having and a not having. It is a possession
and a sense of more to be possessed. The process of
maturation strikes landmarks along the way to indicate what terrain has been covered. Growth as
maturation always casts its eyes around looking for
the way ahead. Hence, growth is an attainment that
is aware of its incompleteness and a provocation to
fresh movement.

All growth is controlled by the goals toward which

it reaches. When the goal is known there is ground for reckoning how one has grown. To have no goal is to have, at best, sporadic, indecisive, inconsequential growth. To have a goal is to have a center which orders and draws life forward.

Growth in grace occurs as life is integrated around the worship of God and the service of the neighbor. Our affections are normally divided and always subject to new diversion, but to grow in our love of God, to love with increasing focus and measure, this is the movement called sanctification. To love our neighbor with increasing sensitivity and caring, this, too, is the movement called sanctification. Sanctification is response to the great commandments: to love God and our neighbor with our whole being. The author of *Theologica Germanica* writes, "Blessedness lies not in much and many, but in One and oneness." [9]

Human life becomes increasingly human—is sanctified—by focused love. To be sanctified is to be in the process of becoming the person we were created to be. For a person to be "godly" means that he or she is maturing into the person God intended; it means that he or she is embodying those qualities of life for which they have gracious potential.

To be in the process of sanctification should make one more sensitive, more receptive, and more giving in the relationship of friend, wife or husband, parent or child. It should make one more able to accept love from others and more able to express love for another. It should bring wholeness of body and spirit, of heart and hand. To be in the process of sanctification should mean that one comes to possess a keen awareness of justice, of the pain of the world, of those who are lost and hungry and exploited. Sanctification should mean a widened sense of our neighbor's need and a renewed strength to serve that need.

Life centered in God and the neighbor releases human experience for rich expansiveness. The effect of this maturation is to open the entire, many-dimensioned person to the many-dimensioned possibilities for life in God. Sanctification is never an achieved status; every actualization of ourselves as persons in relation to God opens new possibilities for further actualization. Maturity always leads to further maturation.

As opposed to so much of what has been historically thought and presently assumed, sanctification is not simply an individual experience. It is not a quality restricted to the solitary person. The holiness of life is found as persons live in Christian community and as persons extend Christian community. The process of sanctification draws one into the binding of life to God and the neighbor. It is in this maturation that our solitariness is shattered and we experience the deepest and most extensive community.

Sanctification does not lead one out of life, away from engagement with its hurt and brokenness. A holy life is a self-giving life. It finds its mode of activity in engagement with human need. Self-cultivation for the purpose of spiritual cosmetics is not allowed, such preening is simply another expression of pride. Sanctification is expressed in giving of ourselves for others; it is a continuous increase in our love for God and love for our neighbor.

And now there remains one final word. The process of sanctification reminds us that our lives are in God's hands. What we experience now is a foretaste of what is to come. God who has begun a good thing in us will bring it to completion in his providence. Holiness is wholeness. Presently we see in part, we experience in part, but we move toward that time when God will bring the fullness of life that will complete his intention for his creation. Then the fragments of our present experience shall be drawn into the wholeness of life in and with God.

CHAPTER NINE

SPEAKING AND LISTENING

God speaks. This is the event which calls faith into being. God speaks. This is the foundation of Christian prayer. The address of God evokes our answering. Only because God has spoken, do persons want to listen and reply.

Through God's grace we are drawn into relationship and made members of God's family. We who were no people are now the people of God (Hosea 1:8-10; 1 Peter 2:10). Prayer is the intimate, personal, unpresuming, yet all-embracing interchange between parent and child. Prayer is family talk.

Urs von Balthazar writes, "Prayer is communion, in which God's word has the initiative and we, at first, are simply listeners. Consequently, what we have to do is, first, listen to God's word and then, through the word, learn how to answer." [10] God's gracious word enables us to hear and understand, to listen and obey, to live and share in the divine life.

The establishment of community sets the context for prayer. What could persons have to say to God had not God already addressed us and given us access to the divine presence. The Elizabethan word for *life* as used in the King James Version is *conversation,* (for example, Philippians 1:27, KJV,

"Only let your conversation be as becometh the gospel of Christ"). Theologically this archaic meaning continues to possess validity. Life is conversation. Life is found in communion with God.

God's speech means Jesus Christ. Jesus is the creative word of love which finds us in our alienation and draws us into new life. We are able to hear God's word because it is spoken in terms which are audible to us. Jesus Christ has assumed our flesh. The incarnation of Jesus Christ says something significant about both God and human beings. The incarnation speaks of the extent of God's self-giving love and the quality of grace. Concerning persons, the incarnation affirms our integrity and worth. God meets us where we are and as we are. The incarnation means that God does not act with abstract sovereignty but in concrete engagement. We are sought as persons for personal relationship. In meeting us as persons, God establishes our humanity in a definitive way; we find our personhood in community with God.

True relationship involves a kind of equality, or at least, an equalization. Professor Austin Farrer writes, "To make a friend of a child I must both be a child with him and also treat him as a grown person. God both descends to us, dealing humanly with his human creatures, and also lifts us to himself. It is by conversing with us that he brings us into conversation." [11] God has become our true parent. We are our truest selves when we learn to listen and speak in prayer.

Speaking and listening are not easy. The quality of relationship is utterly important for communication to take place. Some persons have a fear of hearing. To hear the word of God threatens to bring our present mode of existence under judgment. Human life is too jerry-built, too self-centered to be threatened by a new word of challenge. To hear a word spoken may bring remembrance of the past and of meaning lost. Hearing a word spoken may bring an awareness of the present and of responsibility in an unjust world. Hearing the spoken word may even cast a light on the future and reveal a void. For many there is a fear of listening, since one may hear what one prefers to forget or refuses to appropriate.

To hear the word of the true God always makes us want to escape. It is only idols that we can manipulate and control; it is only false gods to which we can listen with comfort and equanimity. The true God speaks with claim and promise, both of which lead us beyond our native terrain. Consequently, many people do not want to hear God. Hearing brings our life into question or indicates uncertain boundaries.

An act of courage and an understanding of grace are required to say, "Speak, Lord; for thy servant heareth" (1 Samuel 3:9, KJV). We are more likely to identify with the Israelites when they said to Moses, "You speak to us, and we will hear; but let not God speak to us, lest we die" (Exodus 20:19).

It is not easy to listen, especially when the word spoken is God's word. Deafness becomes a defense.

Other people are afraid to speak. At times we

would rather not be heard. We have no desire to talk. To talk is to reveal ourselves, and we do not want to be known as we really are. Silence becomes our fig leaf. The fear of self-knowledge and the fear of being known by others can lead to muteness. On the other hand, we can learn to speak so as to hide; we talk with a strange voice. "He doesn't sound like himself," a friend said of another person.

There are other reasons to be afraid of speaking. What if one cries into a void? What if there is no one to respond? Does one shout to an unhearing world? Sometimes we do not speak because we are not sure that any answer will come. Uncertainty about God can take our tongues. We quiver before the unknown.

Again, there are times we do not speak because we know that we shall be heard. Human relationships are strange, and among their strange qualities is the reluctance we have about sharing our lives. More than anything else we want to share life with others, but more difficult than anything else is the gaining of a freedom which allows us to share life with another. It is as difficult to give to another as it is to receive from another. To share is to risk; to speak carries the possibility of being heard and of being responded to. But what might the response be? With the uncertainties of existence, it is safer to hold what little we now possess than to risk even that meager bit for the hope of a greater promise. Speaking and listening form the character of prayer. But how hard it is to do either. Indeed, it would be impossible if God had not already spoken and were not readily listening for our response. We are able to listen and speak because we have been confronted by grace. Only within the context of grace is the sharing of life possible.

Prayer exposes our condition in life. To be alien to God is reflected in our unwillingness to hear God speak to us, or our unwillingness to speak to God. To be recipient of God's address in Jesus Christ is to know that God's speaking is ultimately a word of love. Our responding is within the community of grace.

To pray is to be in the presence of God. To pray is to both receive and give. To pray is to reach and find one's self being reached for. To pray is not to determine what will happen, only where it will happen—in the presence of the Divine. We are invited into this common life, and we know the urgency of that invitation by Christ's presence in our history. We pray, and faith assumes its flesh.

To be spoken to and to respond is basic to our selfhood. We become aware of ourselves as persons only as we are met by others and engage in dialogue. We become our truest self only as we are met by God and engage in dialogue with him. Persons live in relation with other persons. Only in relationship do we discover our distinctive humanity. Only in relation to God do we discover the deepest dimensions of our personhood.

As persons in relationship with God, we are able to hear and respond; we are able to receive and give. The most direct means of our communication is through speech. We relate to God in a principal way through vocal prayer.

For many Protestants vocal prayer is the only type of prayer we know or practice. In the next chapter we shall attempt to enlarge the understanding of the dimensions of prayer, for the relationship with God encompasses the full range of human possibility for the sharing of life. But it is appropriate to begin with vocal prayer, for speech is the most basic and common form of communication and it is an amazingly rich means of being together.

The functions of speech, as these are generally designated, are expressions of feelings, appeals to other persons, and statements of fact. In vocal prayer all three modes of expression are involved. We offer praise and thanksgiving; we petition God for the needs of life; and we affirm God's presence and providence. Communion through conversation encompasses the full range of life. In prayer, conversation is a natural means of sharing life with God.

Dialogue is effective as there is ability to hear the one who speaks. In human relationships this ability to listen attentatively is as important as the ability to speak clearly. Good listeners are rare, for most people are so aware of themselves, of the impression they are making, of the points they want to argue, and of their interests which must be protected that they simply are not open to other persons. Rather than hearing accurately what another person is saying, we tend to hear them say what we already believe they will say. We limit their possibilities to those we have already come to think they possess. To be able to listen requires a relaxation about ourselves, about our interests, about our status in the relationship.

To affirm that God hears our prayers is to make a major claim about God and God's openness to us. God hears our prayers because he has affirmed his availability to us in Jesus Christ. Such a statement must be made softly and with an appreciation of its magnitude. God, in Jesus Christ, has made himself available to us. We are able to hear God as the Holy Spirit opens our ears and makes us available to God. This thought is humbling. We children of the earth are able to be in relationship with God. It is within the context of grace that we are able to relax about ourselves and we become able to accept ourselves because we have already been accepted by God. We no longer have to pretend; we no longer have to have things come to us in manageable and safe ways. We are opened by God's grace and we are open to God's grace.

To be able to listen to God has a further effect; we are better able to hear other persons. The ability to listen to God gives us the ability to accept ourselves. To be able to listen to God has the effect of establishing a foundation for accepting other persons and allowing them to express themselves in authentic ways. Listening is not a skill; it is reflection of a quality of life. Good listening comes from deep caring.

To hear and speak with God is a way of life within

a special relationship. In prayer we share our lives with God who has shared his life with us.

Prayer calls forth Christian wholeness.

CHAPTER TEN

MEDITATION AND CONTEMPLATION

Simple people of faith as well as the most advanced spiritual guides have often pointed to dimensions of communion with God other than vocal prayer. In the development of Protestant spirituality, however, there has been a tendency to reduce prayer to vocal communication. Prayer is "talking with God." We have affirmed the importance of vocal prayer; now we shall attempt to widen our awareness of other ways to pray.

The two additional forms of prayer mentioned most often are *meditation* and *contemplation*. Both of these dimensions of prayer have been carefully developed and practiced in Roman Catholicism and Eastern Orthodoxy. It is important for those of us outside these traditions to learn about their importance. It is also possible to interpret these dimensions of prayer so that they are congenial to Protestant spirituality.

Meditation has a long tradition of interpretation. One of the classical definitions was given by Hugo of St. Victor in the twelfth century. "Meditation," he says, "is thought concentrated in consideration. It makes careful investigation of the cause and origin, the mode and use, of each single matter that it takes in hand." And again, "Meditation is always occupied with piercing to the core of one particular truth." [12] Perhaps the most influential interpretation of meditation has been that of Ignatius of Loyola, the founder of the Society of Jesus (Jesuits), in his book *Spiritual Exercises.* Loyola defines meditation as conscious, rational concentration upon some specific idea or mental image. He was particularly helpful in utilizing mental pictures, especially of events in the life of Jesus, as a means of aiding the mind's concentration.

Meditation, in all of these definitions, is a form of mental prayer (a name by which it is often called). It works with ideas; it attempts to think through the meaning of a Christian virtue or a quality of God. The chief aim of meditation is to enlighten the mind; it is an effort to gain a vision of truth. This activity is prayer because it is undertaken with a sense of the presence of God and is an effort to think with God about special meaning.

In a moment we shall attempt to interpret meditation in the light of our Protestant heritage as "doing with God." We shall attempt to indicate its possibilities for the enrichment of our practice of prayer.

Contemplation is the other dimension of prayer. There is need for caution in discussion of this form of prayer, for no two contemplatives interpret their experience in exactly the same way. Nevertheless, in its diverse ways, it is as Richard of St. Victor said, "a beholding of God," a beholding which may be described as immediate union, a direct knowledge of, and a complete participation in the life of God. A recent interpreter, Father Shirley Hughson, has described contemplation in a direct and simple way. In the moment of contemplation, he writes, there is "a childlike gaze of love, thinking nought and reasoning nought, but waiting in a complete trust for Him to fill it with Himself, even as when the eye of the body is opened towards the sun, its light floods in and illuminates it to the full." [13]

The experience of contemplation is the experience of unity with God; contemplation is "being with God." And it is the understanding of how one can "be with God" that we shall explore in an effort to make this dimension more readily available for our current spirituality.

Now let us consider each of these types of prayer, first meditation and then contemplation.

Prayer must always be understood in terms of relationship. To pray is to be in relationship with God, and prayer is an adventure of exploring the possible facets of meaningful relationship. There is no clear line between activities within a relationship, likewise there is no clear line between meditation and contemplation. Meditation, as we have described it, is "doing with God"; and contemplation is "being with God." Meditation represents a more active mode and contemplation a more receptive mode in the divine-human relationship.

To meditate is "to do" something with God. To interpret meditation in this way is to enlarge it beyond mental prayer, but it does keep a distinctive character of this experience as it has been traditionally described. An analogy from human relations may be helpful. It is a common phenomenon that two people in love often find that their relationship does not progress as fast when they simply look at each other as when they look at something else, some third object, together. A common focus draws two persons together in subtle but firm ways. Such unity is vividly realized when people who enjoy music listen together, when people who enjoy art look together, when parents tend their children together, or when two religious persons worship together. What began as two persons doing something in common ends with the participants recognizing a resulting closeness.

There is the same possibility in the relationship of persons with God in prayer. Prayer may be the experience of "doing with God." Meditation occurs when we read, or think, or listen, or look, or work with God.

Prayer can take place when we relax and think with God. For instance, we might take an idea, such as peace, and think about it with God. We can explore its meaning, its application, its practical possibilities, and our responsibility in its service. One could do the same thing with any similar notion such as grace, or joy, or justice.

Prayer can take place when we become actively engaged in life with God. We might undertake a task and execute it with a sense of doing it with God. One might work in the political arena. One might do physical labor. One might stand by those who are oppressed, or one might work to feed the hungry. Think about it—"meals on wheels" can be an activity of prayer. Working on legislation can be an activity of prayer. Raising money for a good cause can be an activity of prayer. In any of these activities we can endeavor to be "doing with God." As we work together, communion is experienced.

Too often prayer becomes an introverted concern for ourselves. We concentrate upon our own selves; we check our spiritual pulse; we care about our spiritual cosmetics; and we talk about our spiritual condition. Not only is there a danger of "an indecent exposure of the ego" as William James suggested, there is a danger of concentrating too much upon ourselves. St. Teresa of Jesus once remarked that one can make more spiritual progress in contemplating our Lord for five minutes than by contemplating ourselves for thirty minutes. And one might add, at times we can make more spiritual progress in being engaged with our Lord in a common task than by talking with God.

Once again, prayer can take place when we undertake every activity with a sense of engaging it with God. Dr. Frank Laubach is a prime example of a person who attempted to keep an awareness of God in all of his activities; he learned in our time to practice the presence of God. Dr. Laubach says, in *Letters by a Modern Mystic,* that he made an effort to let every conversation, every letter, every chance meeting, every activity become an expression of prayer for the person he met, the cause he was serving, the activity he was doing. To meditate does not mean to be abstracted from the world; it is to live within a relationship that affects the ordinariness of our daily rounds. Thomas Hardy remarks in his novel *The Return of the Native,* "Persons with any weight of character carry, like planets, their atmosphere along with them in their orbits." [14] Persons of spiritual weight carry their sense of the presence of God. Whether in study or physical work, in play or at rest, we are alive to God's presence and are alive to engage life with him.

Meditation may find validity for us as a form of prayer as we learn how to practice the presence of God as we engage in service to the world.

Contemplation is also a dimension of relationship. We have called contemplation "being with God." Sometimes the deepest community is not found in talking or in doing but simply in being with another person, sitting in their presence, quietly enjoying their company.

Perhaps you have had the experience of hiking in the mountains when suddenly you came upon a beautiful scene. Up to this time you have been busy walking and perhaps talking with companions, now suddenly you reach a place where an awesome panorama comes into view. At such a moment you do not want to talk or move on; it is enough simply to "be there." There is no desire to use the beauty. You do not even ask questions such as: How far do you guess we can see? or could we build a tourist trail here? or How many board-feet do you think are in that forest? In such a moment you do not ask any questions, or even consciously desire to "meditate." You are satisfied to wait, receive, and enjoy. We can experience God in this way. The experience may be only for a moment, or it may extend over a period of time. It is important, for in that moment you are with God, and you are content to "be with God."

At the level of human relationships there are similar experiences. In friendship or love there may occur moments when one does not want to talk with the other person. There are even moments when one person does not wish to do anything with the other person. You are happy just to be with the other. In fact, there are times in good relationships when communication takes place in silence. One knows a sense of well-being, of joy, of significant sharing by being in the presence of the other person. To attempt to describe, to talk about, to analyze, or to reflect upon the meaning found tends to destroy the experience.

A student came in from a date. "How did things go?" his roommate asked. "Great." "So, tell me about it." As the student began to talk, he knew that he could not describe the experience or what the meaning had been, and he knew that as he tried to describe it the very effort was making him lose its meaning. Some things just cannot be talked about.

So in prayer it is possible to be with God, to wait silently in the divine presence, to know the reality of God with us, and to relax into that special communion. There is no desire to analyze or describe or make anything else of that relationship other than to enjoy being in it. In that experience there is a movement of our total person to the totality of God; we are in direct, immediate relation with God.

Such an experience cannot be controlled or forced; it cannot be set on a timetable or come as the result of even the most faithful following of a formula. One can be receptively alive, ready to respond, and sensitively searching. These moments are moments of grace. They come at times—often unexpected times—within the relationship with God when gift and reception interact in spontaneous fulfillment.

How can one describe such a quality of relationship? In basic ways it is impossible; yet we want to communicate something of its meaning. Some persons have cautiously attempted to indicate what the contemplative experience may be. Friedrich Schleiermacher over a century ago made such an effort.

> Did I venture to compare it, seeing I cannot describe it, I would say it is fleeting and transparent as the vapour which the dew breathes on blossom and fruit, it is bashful and tender as a maiden's kiss, it is holy and fruitful as a bridal embrace. Nor is it merely like, it is all this. It is the first contact of the universal life with the individual. It fills no time and fashions nothing palpable. It is the holy wedlock of the Universe with the incarnated Reason for a creative, productive embrace. It is immediate, raised above all error and misunderstanding. You lie directly on the bosom of the infinite world. In that moment, you are its soul.[15]

It is necessary to stress that this occurs in a relationship. It is something which happens to a person, something which at times can come as a light wind and other times as a violent storm. Such a relation may be hardly noticed, or it may completely control our sensibility. Person meets person—the divine Person encounters us as persons, and "person is lost in person without losing personality." [16]

During contemplation one is simply "being with God." There is a full sharing, a silent exchange of love.

It would be wrong to set an ascending scale and say that each type of prayer should lead to a higher level, so one moves through vocal prayer, to meditation, to contemplation. In relationships every meeting is important, and each is important in its own time and way. Nonetheless, for those of us who have been raised in the Protestant tradition, there is need to explore some of the dimensions of prayer which express other aspects of relationship than talking with God. We should move on to appropriate forms of "doing with God" and of "being with God."

In exploring different forms of prayer, we can find fresh dimensions to Christian wholeness.

CHAPTER ELEVEN

EXCELLENCE AND HUMILITY

Jesus tells a parable. A Pharisee and a publican go to the temple to pray. One speaks of his religiosity and his moral worth; the other could not lift his eyes because of an overwhelming sense of unworthiness. The Pharisee, aware of his own quality, thanks God that he is not like the publican. Then Jesus comments that, nonetheless, it is the publican, the one who confesses his sin, who is justified (Luke 18:9-14). We hear the story, then thank God that we are not like the Pharisee.

So the subtlety of pride continues its pervasive corruption. The parable on the other hand provokes many thoughts. What is the place of moral striving in Christian life? What value should be given to the embodiment of moral worth? Should the Christian set goals of excellence? What sort of excellence? And, what of humility? Can humility which becomes self-aware retain its character?

Jesus draws the conclusion: "Every one who exalts himself will be humbled, but he who humbles himself will be exalted" (Luke 18:14). Excellence and humility, is there room for both? Are they two sides of the same reality?

There are New Testament injunctions which exhort disciples of Jesus to both virtues. On the one hand, there is excellence. "And I will show you a still more excellent way" (1 Corinthians 12:31). "Approve what is excellent" (Philippians 1:10).

On the other hand, there is humility. "Clothe yourselves, all of you, with humility toward one another, for 'God opposes the proud, but gives grace to the humble' " (1 Peter 5:5).

We are called to excellence. It is a Christian virtue to aspire to excel in goodness. The call of God also evokes humility, and we kneel in awe before God's sovereign glory.

Excellence denotes a superlative. For human life, excellence means becoming all that one is created to be. Such self-finding is a gift as well as a demand; it is a quality of relationship offered by God and a quality of relationship demanded in our interaction with others. Excellence in Christian living is love, love for God and for one another. To set this goal challenges us from spiritual mediocrity and points us beyond restricted vision, satisfied achievement, and small-hearted living.

Christian excellence is a reflection of God's grace. The fruits of the Spirit are the result of the nurture of God's presence. God's grace graces human life. Grace makes life gracious. So Paul speaks, "The fruit of the Spirit is love, joy, peace, patience, kindness, goodness, faithfulness, gentleness, self-control; against such there is no law" (Galatians 5:22-23).

We are led to the "more excellent way" of love (1 Corinthians 12:31). Paul's depiction of love is not simply the result of the apostle's ruminations about the word *love* or possible ways in which this quality may be expressed. 1 Corinthians 13 is a meditation on the cross. It is an effort to describe the love of God in Jesus Christ and what, consequently, it should mean in Christian living. Perhaps this is most clear in the central passage. "Love bears all things, believes all things, hopes all things, endures all things. Love never ends" (1 Corinthians 13:7-8a).

This is the excellence of God in Christ. As Christians we are called to excellence. We are called to bear and believe and hope and endure with Christ. Not to serve God with the intention to serve fully is to fail to pursue the way of excellence. The call to excellence is a call to shatter our pretension of faithfulness and inculcate the fullness of love and service.

Excellence implies a breadth of inclusiveness as well as a depth of quality. All of life is to be given to God. "I appeal to you therefore, brethren, by the mercies of God, to present your bodies as a living sacrifice, holy and acceptable to God, which is your spiritual worship" (Romans 12:1).

All of life and the finest aspects of life are from God and are to be God's. Excellence is found as one pursues from among all of the possibilities the one greatest value. It is to have a single will and a focused love. Excellence is seeing God and our neighbor first of all and caring for them most of all.

Excellence means the actualization of our created potential for intellectual strength, for moral goodness, for sensitive awareness, and for emotional richness. Excellence is neither a state of being nor a possession. It is the following of a way, a process of growth that involves constant challenge and renewal.

The movement toward excellence is difficult. An anonymous writer of a church school publication has expressed the drive:

> Keep me from turning back!
> My hand is on the plough, my faltering hand;
> But all in front of me is untilled land,
> The wilderness and solitary place,
> The lonely desert with its interspace.
>
> The handles of my plough with tears are wet,
> The shares with rust are spoiled—and yet—
>   and yet—
> My God! My God! Keep me from turning back.

Jesus embodies excellence. Yet Jesus represents a strange turning of value, for in the life of Jesus we find excellence expressed in crucifixion. Excellence and crucifixion—this is an almost unimaginable conjunction. The point, however, is unmistakable in Jesus' ministry: Excellence is found in servanthood. Full life occurs in the full giving of life. Jesus, "Who, though he was in the form of God, did not count equality with God a thing to be grasped, but emptied himself, taking the form of a servant, being born in the likeness of men. And being found in human form he humbled himself and became obedient unto death, even death on a cross" (Philippians 2:6-8).

Now we reach a cardinal point: Excellence is expressed as humility.

Humility is a quality of life appropriate to the presence of God. We are given humility; humility is not an achievement. We are humbled by God's glory, by God's goodness, by God's grace and forgiveness.

Awareness of who we are before God is the necessary door to excellence. In his book *The Steps of Humility,* Saint Bernard of Clairvaux speaks of the qualities of Christian life. He finds humility to be the initial and the final virtue. Humility is among the most immediate, the most spontaneous, and the most simple of Christian qualities. It is also among the most impressive, the richest, and the most profound of Christian virtues.

In Christian experience, goodness seldom sees itself as such. Personal strength does not focus upon its own resources. Humility contemplates God and not itself.

Humility is not weakness. It is a recognition of God as God, and it is the recognition of our personhood under God. Humility is the door to strength; it is the submersion of the self to the cause served. Jesus, who humbled himself, set the way and invites his disciples to follow. "Take my yoke upon you, and learn from me; for I am gentle and lowly in heart" (Matthew 11:29).

Will the meek really inherit the earth? Jesus says so, but it seems impossible. The meek are used, taken advantage of, stepped on, or passed by. Yet we have our Lord's word. Perhaps the meek inherit the earth, that is, the true earth which only the meek can recognize for its value. Perhaps the meek inherit the earth because they see it as God's gift and embrace it with joy. Only the meek know that the earth cannot be possessed but that it can be loved and lived with, enjoyed and utilized for common good. The meek inherit the earth because the rough hands of capricious self-interest cannot ultimately hold or force the earth. In the last analysis the earth is the Lord's and those who wait with him find its meaning. They enjoy its beauty. They discover its possibility. They are thankful for its gifts.

Humility and excellence are indissoluble. Each expresses the other. How shall the dynamic be stated?

When I am willing to be set aside or used for the gospel; when I am willing to say, He must increase, but I must decrease—that is humility and that is excellence.

When I seek God's will and not my own well-being, when I take from God's hand whatever he has to give with a happy heart attached to the Giver and not to the gift—that is humility and that is excellence.

When I know that my life is within the context of God's grace, and I live as one who claims nothing but possesses everything—that is humility and that is excellence.

When I go into the world as one who seeks to be neighbor to every person I meet and the next person I meet—that is humility and that is excellence.

When I am able to say, My God and my all— that is humility and that is excellence.

Humility and excellence, both are preeminent virtues, and both are tempted to pride. Excellence is tempted by the pride of achievement. Humility is tempted by the pride of self-denial. Unwholesome pride can subtly commandeer wholesome virtue whether of self-affirmation or self-renunciation. Pride claims as achievement what is a gift from God.

To be humble is to live with constant awareness of our dependence upon grace. To strive for excellence is to utilize the resources provided by grace.

Excellence and humility, so often divided, are complementary in Christian wholeness.

CHAPTER TWELVE

BOREDOM AND BEATITUDE

Clifton Fadiman has described our time as one of a special kind of boredom, "Not unhappiness, not fatigue . . . but that odd modern *stunned* look that comes from a surfeit of toys and a deficiency of thoughts." [17]

Each of us has seen and experienced this modern dispiriting; it is around us and within us. The lackluster face of the pedestrian on the streets of Seattle and Richmond, of St. Petersburg and San Francisco, Phoenix and Chicago. The vacant stare, the superficial laughter, the dogged motion and the too quick reaction. We look into expressionless faces and casually note unexpectant countenances. We dream of so much and settle for so little; we talk of large meaning and accept the pittance of the moment. We race from event to event and push ourselves to greet and wave. There is the animated talk of the cocktail party, the church social, and the club convention — and deep within we know that it is all a cover-up of boredom.

Karl Heim has spoken of the "serene secularist," that is the person who asks no ultimate questions and who does not ask why he or she does not ask ultimate questions. We live within the confines of everydayness and have no holes punched in the low canopy of our horizons.

Only a short time ago Paul Tillich used to ask, "What is your ultimate concern?" To ask that question of a random sample of people on the street, or walking on a campus, or sitting behind a desk in an office, or working at home on dinner and dishes would bring only a puzzled stare, a bewildered gaze.

Several years ago I was speaking to a group of law students. I was using as an illustration of life a trip on an ocean liner. I described life on the ship as good, with food, freedom, entertainment, fellow passengers, and lack of immediate responsibility (life very much as we middle-class Americans experience it). But, I suggested, occasionally some one walks out to the bow of the ship, looks across the water, and wonders where the ship is headed. When the session was over, a student came to me and said without great feeling and in a matter-of-fact way, "I had never thought of that question before. I wonder why you think it is important?" He was not fighting the issue; he was simply registering a mild puzzlement. He was, I assumed, a serene secularist.

We must not too simply put down such an attitude. Religious interpreters have at times reinforced adoption of society's values and visions. Popular preachers have enjoined persons to adjust to life, to seek their happiness in immediate self-interest, to find their meaning in possessions and popularity. And it is tempting when one lives in a privileged place, such as the United States, to have a sense of sufficiency and slip into the doldrums of boredom.

It is typical of our time to find persons who have achieved rather well, who have gained most of the things they once thought were necessary to the good life, and who now find that in having what they want they do not want what they have.

In a small North Carolina town, I was visiting in the home of a middle-aged couple. They called some friends to come over, and soon there were twenty odd people gathered. These were all friends and members of a social circle. After general small talk one of the couples said to the others, "We want to tell you something. We are going to separate." There was a register of surprise; then the woman said, "It isn't that anything special is wrong. It is just that there is no longer any meaning. Our children are in college, and we have developed different interests. We are living separate lives anyway." Others began to talk, and over half of the couples said that they were in the same situation. Economically they were successful; socially they were in an active group. They attended church, basketball games, and horse shows. But inwardly there was an emptiness, a void, a deep sense of isolation, a lack of meaning for and in life.

Too often we are bored. Not so much tired, we can still run and do and talk and party and stay busy with busy things, but we are bored. The running has no meaning; the doing is too shallow; there is no fulfillment. We become bored with our friends, with our families, with ourselves. Life has bottomed out, and the bottom is only skin-deep.

Soren Kierkegaard, as he begins *Either/Or,* comments, "Boredom is the root of all evil. . . . All men are bores . . . Those who do not bore themselves are generally people who, in one way or another, keep themselves extremely busy; these people are precisely on this account the most tiresome, the most utterly unendurable." It is such boredom that is an expression of despair and which issues in a "sickness unto death." [18]

Such a description of contemporary experience is only one among many possible options. Life, actual human life, is a complex tangle of reaction and meaning, of hopes and values. At times it seems almost impossible to speak of human nature in a general or common sense manner, for people are at many different places with many different histories, present conditions, and future expectations. Nonetheless, one of the dominant aspects of contemporary life is a sense of its lack of quality, its failure to produce significance, the lack of growth in relationships, and a sense of incompleteness.

Perhaps in such a context of boredom, it is worthwhile, once again, to reflect on the notion of beatitude or blessedness. What goes into making life blessed? What is the meaning of blessedness?

It is clear from the beatitudes of Jesus' teaching (Matthew 5:3-11; Luke 6:20-22) that the condition of beatitude is not dependent upon external circumstances, for those who experience blessedness are the hungry, the mourners, the persecuted, the reviled, and the hated. Blessedness comes from a rootage of life which is deeper than the vicissitudes of existence. Blessedness derives from a relationship with God which is stronger and more enduring than the relation to the external conditions of society. It comes to those who love God first and serve God faithfully. Blessedness comes to the poor in spirit who are pure in heart, to those who hunger and thirst after righteousness and seek peace in human affairs.

The blessedness of which Jesus speaks is not happiness. *Happiness,* as it is usually understood, is too pale a word to carry the meaning Jesus intends. Perhaps *joy* is a more accurate word. True joy comes from the deepest recesses of our lives and moves through us thoroughly and overflows from us. Joy is the satisfaction of life which knows that our relationship with God is good, that it is strong, and that it is growing.

Joy is the result of grace in human life. Our present is created by God's presence, and we know that our lives are hidden with Christ in the divine reality. Joy or blessedness comes from communion with God.

One meaning of the word *salvation* is "being made whole," that is, life is made complete. The word *salvation* means healing, and it comes from the same Latin root as the word *salve,* an ointment which heals cuts and abrasions. Consequently "to be saved" is to be made whole; it is to be healed and have life made what it was intended to be in God's creation.

For Christians, the relating of God to us and our relating to God is accomplished by God's coming to our side in Jesus Christ. So with Charles Wesley we can say of Jesus, "Thy name salvation is." The salvation which Jesus brings is wholeness. The Gospel of John emphasizes this purpose as it quotes Jesus, "I came that they may have life, and have it abundantly" (John 10:10).

Our incompleteness, our boredom comes with being estranged from God. Broken relationship leaves us with a dispirited emptiness, with a sense of lostness, and with a frantic grasping of whatever is available. To be out of community with God is to be in need of healing. We may have a surfeit of toys, but we carry a sense of incompleteness and are in search of meaning.

Salvation comes, bringing with it wholeness and joy. Salvation means blessedness.

In the Old Testament one meaning of the word *righteous* is that a thing is used for the purpose for which it was created. In this sense one might speak of any instrument as being righteous if it fulfills its purpose. For instance, a chair might be called righteous if one can sit comfortably and securely in it. Or one might call a bow righteous if one can shoot it straight and with power. Persons are called righteous if they fulfill the purpose for which they were created, if they live in vital relation with God.

Boredom can issue into blessedness as Christ claims us, and life which has been broken begins to discover the possibilities of wholeness.

CHAPTER THIRTEEN

DEATH AND RESURRECTION

Death is upon us, and not simply in the personal sense that each of us is faced with the reality of our own death. Our contemporary culture is death-stained and death-concerned. The reality of death may be fascinating or frightening, the result of human sin or caused by natural processes or disordered disaster. Death may be the source of either guilt or release; it may be an expression of genocide or national or personal self-interest. Death may come as the final enemy or as a friend.

Two prominent ideas about personal death have dominated recent discussion. For some, death is a closing out, an annulment, the end of meaning. From this reality there is no exit, and it promises no positive significance. To die is to have life brought to an end and its value come to a close.

Tom Stoppard says in *Rosencrantz & Guildenstern Are Dead,* "Death is not anything, death is not . . . it's the absence of presence, nothing more . . . a gap you can't see, and when the wind blows through it, it makes no sound. . . ." [19]

Not everyone who views death in this way yields to pessimism. Such an awareness of the finality of death may be discouraging or lead to cynicism and despair. But it may also enhance the present, place a premium upon the actual experiences of life. Death as the end may direct the search for meaning to the relationships in which persons live, the jobs presently done, hopes for immediate realization. To recognize that there is no exodus from life to life can produce a profound debility of spirit, but it may produce intense effort to make the most of the present.

For others, death is an access, a transition into a more significant future, an entrance into new dimensions of life. Again this belief may have opposite effects. It may lead to a devaluing of the present, to an acquiescence with whatever is, to a life directed only toward the future. Or it may, on the contrary, lead to an affirmation of life as a continuum: The present has meaning as a partner with the future. Such an understanding of life may set a large context for everydayness, a context which produces confidence and courage.

In malignant and merciful ways, death stalks us. The reality that life is coming to an end is the reality with which we live and with which we must learn to cope. Our understanding of the nature of death sets the possibilities for the way in which we face this climatic moment. The Roman philosopher Seneca drew these two dominant themes together: "Death either destroys or unhusks us. If it means liberation, better things await us when our burden's gone; if destruction, nothing at all awaits us; blessings and curses are abolished." [20]

In recent years there has been much interest in the actual event of dying. There are collections of reports on the experiences people have in the process of dying, such as Raymond A. Moody has gathered and Elizabeth Kubler-Ross has explored. Courses on death and dying are popular on college campuses and in church groups. Death is a prominent subject in medical and legal discussions; interest has even invaded the conversations of coffee breaks.

But all of this general interest and daily talk fails to deflect the full impact of death when it knocks on the door of our home. "It is as natural to die as to be born," Francis Bacon claimed. Such a word is too cool for many who face the power of death. Recently I was talking with a person who has been constant in talking about and teaching about death. Then a Mother died. "I thought I was ready," was the only comment that could come through the anguish.

Death surprises us. We are seldom ready for the moment when death comes. All that has been done, all that might be done sweep by us in a flash of joy, dismay, frustration, and hope.

There is another dimension which we often fail to take with full strength as we discuss death and dying, that is, the fact of mass death, of horrible, unbelievable human suffering and destruction. We so often limit our discussion of death to old age, to privileged life, and fulfilled opportunities. We think of death in individual and solitary ways. When we face the reality, I shall die, there is a trembling of the knees and an awakening of our sense. But the reality of death cuts across human experience and often in senseless, ruinous ways. There is the holocaust, the famine in Honan Province in China in 1943 when some five million persons died; and in the last few years there have been Bangladesh and the southern Sahara. In every country there are terrible, needless deaths, such as is found in the slums of Washington and Toronto, of Rio de Janeiro and Cuernavaca, of Calcutta and Manila, and which are found through the rural areas of the world.

To consider death not only drives us inward, it should also drive us outward. To think of death is to think of justice and corporate selfishness, of production and distribution; to think of death necessarily reveals the binding together of all human life and raises fundamental questions of good and evil.

On the human level, which is our level and the first level on which we must engage life, we face the unexpectedness and the tragedy of death in a multitude of ways. For instance, we may be simply self-interested: What is my destiny? We may attempt to remove death's annuling power by busyness with ordinary life as Tolstoy poignantly described in *The Death of Ivan Illych.* Just recently a friend called to talk of her father's funeral and then spoke of a *bon voyage* party she was giving for a friend who was taking a trip (perhaps there is a double possibility of meaning). This was not insensitivity; it was a means of dealing with death by plunging earnestly into life.

Others face death by attempting to create continuing memorials for the one who has died. So we attempt to preserve the meaning of life beyond a limited human span through institutions and projects which will continue a name and a spirit. Such activity may represent guilty pretention or authentic gratitude, and only in specific cases can the motive be determined.

Again, emotions of hurt, loneliness, guilt, love distress, and expectation may be released through prayer or crying, through conversation or silent sharing. The range of reaction to death is a wide and as varied as the persons who feel the reaper's blade and that is as wide as the human family.

Joseph Addison gave a perceptive description of the way in which persons faced death two centuries ago in *The Spectator*. "The end of man's life is often compared to the winding up of a well-written play, where the principal persons still act in character, whatever the fate is which they undergo." [21]

The reality of death is with us. We face it as and who we are. It is at this juncture that those who are Christians, those who are in Christ, reveal their faith which is their character.

"Death", Dietrich Bonhoeffer wrote in his *Letters and Papers From Prison,* "is the supreme festival on the road to freedom." Such confidence in death as access to the fuller presence of God can only come from a conviction that our lives are hidden with Christ in God—with Christ who is the incarnation of persisting, caring grace—and in God who is the sovereign Lord of life before and beyond death.

In Dostoevsky's great novel *The Brothers Karamazov,* one of the brothers, Alyosha, is a saintly figure. He is a believer in the midst of a life which would tend to make belief facetious if not impossible. In a series of experiences he meets a group of boys whose leader Kolya is precocious in intellect and in destructive hate. A victim of their cruelty is Ilusha, a small, sick boy who finally dies. The experience of suffering and now death brings a somber recognition of destructive finality. Then, with a hope that comes only after hopelessness has been faced, there takes shape a new vision.

> "Karamazov," cried Kolya, "can it be true what's taught us in religion, that we shall all rise again from the dead and shall live and see each other again, all, Ilusha too?"

> "Certainly we shall all rise again, certainly we shall see each other and shall tell each other with joy and gladness all that has happened!" Alyosha answered, half laughing, half enthusiastic.[22]

Certainly! This is an affirmation of faith; it has been won for those who are Christians by the way in which God in Christ went through the crucible of death and established, through sovereign power, the fact of resurrection.

Resurrection, in the Christian tradition, is not understood as built upon our human nature. It is not a necessary quality of our personhood, and it is not based upon values which we possess in ourselves as human beings. Resurrection is a possibility and a reality because of God's grace. It represents a new creative act in which God calls forth life and affirms the meaning of our existence. To be resurrected with Christ is to be given new being and to be brought into an enduring relationship through the constancy of God's grace.

For the Christian, death has no dominion. The kingdom and the power and the glory are God's and we are God's. The movement of the Christian life is to die with Christ and to be resurrected with Christ.

> Do you not know that all of us who have been baptized into Christ Jesus were baptized into his death? We were buried therefore with him by baptism into death, so that as Christ was raised from the dead by the glory of the Father, we too might walk in newness of life. For if we have been united with him in a death like his, we shall certainly be united with him in a resurrection like his (Romans 6:3-5).

Certainly! Once again an affirmation of faith.

Death is tragic. It is a terrible experience—whether we speak of spiritual or physical death. We want to protect ourselves against its onslaught. But it is in dying to ourselves that we become alive in Christ. It is through physical death that we enter into the new and fulfilling relationship of resurrection.

The renewal of life is a gift of grace.

There is a basic sense in which resurrection with Christ is a present reality, an already realized condition. To be in Christ is to be alive to God; it is already to experience the quality of relationship which death cannot annul. To be in Christ is to lose the sting of the fear of death. To have new being in

Jesus Christ is to live as resurrected and in anticipation of resurrection. It is to experience the relationship which will continue beyond death and finally prove the ultimate reality of God's sovereign providence.

But there is another dimension of overcoming death through resurrection, namely, to possess life is to share life. To possess life is to enter the struggle with the principalities and powers which destroy life and especially to take responsibility for the struggle against human sinfulness which so cruelly decimates human existence. To be in Christ is to be placed in opposition to all unnecessary death and all limitation of human possibility for full life. To be living as resurrected is to serve the cause of life.

Within the Christian context, physical death is not the greatest evil. There are things worse than physical death. There are also things worth dying for. In much contemporary talk there seems to be a premium placed upon merely staying alive. It is as though survival is more significant than the quality of life. But the love of God and the service of the neighbor is a greater good than physical survival. Earnest Gordon in his account of life in a concentration camp in Southeast Asia, *Through the Valley of Kwai,* tells of the heroism of a Scots soldier. The Japanese commander had the prisoners' shovels counted and the count came up one short. Convinced that the prisoners had confiscated the shovel, he asked who had stolen it. No one answered. Then the commander ordered his men to shoot the prisoners one by one until someone confessed. The Scots soldier stepped forward and confessed and was shot to death. On recounting the shovels, it was discovered that they were all there—the guards had miscounted.

There are things more important than physical death; integrity, faithfulness, service, love of God, and love of neighbor are among these values. When death is seen as access to the fuller relationship with God, there is a release from the fear of death. This is not to deny that there is keenness of loss, or that we do not know that more and better things might have been done with life. But the Christian faces death confident in the grace of God.

Death and resurrection, both are a part of the Christian's experience. It is in going through death to resurrection that one discovers the wholeness of life.

CONCLUSION

Remember the faith that took men from home
At the call of a wandering preacher.
Our age is an age of moderate virtue
And of moderate vice
When men will not lay down the Cross
Because they will never assume it.
Yet nothing is impossible, nothing,
To men of faith and conviction.
Let us therefore make perfect our will.
O God, help us.[23]

T.S. Eliot

Life is a pilgrimage. Would to God the calms on life's voyage would last, Herman Melville cries, but "calms are crossed by storms." Then Melville goes on to comment: "There is no steady unretracing progress in this life; we do not advance through fixed gradations, and at the last one pause." [24]

So the search for Christian wholeness is a finding and a new questing; it is not possession but being possessed; it knows temptation and failure, but it also knows grace and new beginning.

NOTES

1. Alfred Lord Tennyson, "In Memoriam," *The Works of Alfred Lord Tennyson* (New York: The Macmillan Company, 1961), p. 285.

2. Langston Hughes, "A Dream Deferred," *The Panther and The Lash: Poems of Our Times (New York: Alfred A. Knopf, Inc., 1951), by permission of Alfred A. Knopf, Inc.*

3. *The Proposed Book of Confessions* (Atlanta, Ga.: Materials Distribution Service, The Presbyterian Church in the United States, 1976), pp. 170-171.

4. William Shakespeare, *King Henry VI*, Part II, Act III, sc. 2.

5. Edward Connery Lathem, ed., "Revelation," *The Poetry of Robert Frost* Copyright 1934, © 1969 by Holt, Rinehart and Winston. Copyright © 1962 by Robert Frost. Reprinted by permission of Holt, Rinehart and Winston, publishers.

6. Prayer of Confession Number 727, *The Methodist Hymnal* (Nashville: The Methodist Publishing House, 1964).

7. Alfred North Whitehead, *Science and the Modern World* (New York: The Macmillan Company, 1925), p. 276.

8. E. C. Hoskyns and F. N. Davey, *The Fourth Gospel,* 2nd ed. rev. (London: Faber and Faber, 1947), p. 5.

9. Susan Winkworth, trans., *Theologica Germanica* (London: Macmillan & Co., 1874), p. 28.

10. Urs Von Balthazar, *Prayer,* trans. A. V. Littledale (London: Geoffrey Chapman, 1961), p. 19.

11. Austin Farrer, *Lord, I Believe* (London: The Faith Press, Ltd., 1958), p. 19.

12. Kenneth E. Kirk, *The Vision of God* (London: Longman's Press, 1931), p. 375.

13. Shirley Hughson, *Contemplative Prayer* (New York: The Macmillan Company, 1935), p. 57.

14. Thomas Hardy, *The Return of the Native* (New York: Harper & Brothers Publishers, 1878), p. 35.

15. John Oman, trans., *Speeches on Religion* (New York: Harper & Row Publishers, 1958), p. 43.

16. P. T. Forsyth, *The Soul of Prayer* (London: Independent Press, 1949), p. 45.

17. Clifton Fadiman, *Any Number Can Play* (New York: World Publishing Company, 1957), p. 15.

18. Robert Bretall, ed., *A Kierkegaard Anthology* (Princeton, New Jersey: Princeton University Press, 1946), pp. 22-24.

19. Tom Stoppard, *Rosencrantz & Guildenstern Are Dead* (New York: Grove Press, Inc., 1967), p. 124. Used by permission of the publishers.

20. Seneca, "Letters to Lucillius" (1st Century, Letter XXIII) *Seneca's Morals* (New York: Lowell, Lowell, Inc.), pp. 326-327.

21. Joseph Addison, *The Works of Joseph Addison,* vol. 3 as quoted in *The Spectator* (London: George Bell and Sons, 1906), p. 340.

22. Fyodor Dostoevsky, *The Brothers Karamazov* (New York: The Macmillan Company, 1926), p. 838.

23. T. S. Eliot, "Choruses from 'The Rock,' " *Collected Poems 1909-1962* (New York: Harcourt Brace Jovanovich, Inc., 1963). Reprinted by permission of the publishers.

24. Herman Melville, *Moby Dick* (New York: Albert & Charles Boni, Inc., 1935), p. 435.

A STUDY GUIDE

by Thomas A. Langford III *

INTRODUCTION

Christian living is a biography full of tensions and seeming contradictions. Christians live in a world which must be affirmed and also denied. We remember the past, live in the present, and look toward the future. We proclaim that the kingdom of God is present but not yet complete, and we worship a Lord who has died and yet still lives.

Such a life is not easy. There are no simple answers for dealing with the challenges of the Christian life. **Christian Wholeness** is the study of the complexities which are found in actual Christian living. This book shows how through complementary virtues the Christian's life develops. This study guide is written to aid in the discussion of this book. It is intended to lead your study group in an exploration of the tensions involved in Christian living.

METHOD

This study guide is written to cover six study sessions of sixty to ninety minutes each. The guide fol-

---

*The study guide for the book was prepared by Thomas A. Langford III , son of the author, and minister of the Royal Oaks United Methodist Church, Kannapolis, North Carolina. A graduate of Davidson College and Duke Divinity School, he is serving his first appointment in the Western North Carolina Annual Conference.

lows the outline of **Christian Wholeness** and is written to study from one to three chapters of the book at each meeting. It is intended to provide basic questions as a means to begin group discussion. This guide does not attempt to ask all the questions prompted by each chapter. Your own questions may be better. The questions are to help you explore the depth and height of the Christian life. Use this guide only as it aids your discussion of the issues which are important to you.

A study group of eight to twelve members seems to be an ideal size. There are several requirements which should be stressed. Each member should be responsible (a) to read the chapters and study questions for each lesson prior to the meeting; (b) to think carefully about the material; and (c) to be willing to participate in the discussion. A commitment by each person to be present at each of the six lessons has also been found to be useful in such groups. It seems best to have the same leader for the whole study. The task of the leader is to lead the discussion, to participate openly and honestly, to encourage all members to join the discussion, to outline the work to be done prior to the next meeting, and to open and close each session with time of prayer.

As a final note, **Christian Wholeness** can best be understood and studied when each group member is committed to understanding the book's relevance in his or her own life. The book speaks of tensions and struggles. As each member reflects upon his or her own journey toward Christian wholeness and shares this pilgrimage with the group, the member will be drawn more into the richness of the Christian experience. That is the goal of both the book and this study guide.

SESSION ONE

BACKGROUND MATERIAL

Introduction; Chapter One; *Self-Giving And Self-Finding;* Chapter Two: *Liberation and Celebration*

QUESTIONS

1. "Christian living is a struggle for wholeness. Wholeness of vision, wholeness of experience, wholeness of relationships, and wholeness of service are all necessary components of Christian maturation." The book begins with these words. But the Christian life is filled with many tensions. After looking at the table of contents: Where are the particular tensions which you are now experiencing in your life? Do these tensions hurt or help you in your search for Christian wholeness? Do you believe that Christian wholeness is an achievable goal? How would you describe or illustrate a life of Christian wholeness?

2. Read: Matthew 10:39   Discipleship
   13:44-6   Parables of the Kingdom
   16:24-6   Discipleship
   Mark   8:34-6   Discipleship
   Luke   9:23-5   Discipleship
   17:33   Discipleship

Self-giving and self-finding is a central theme in the New Testament. How does this compare to the contemporary emphasis upon self-assertiveness? Have there been times in your life when you have found yourself through self-giving? How might this self-giving → self-finding model become more common in your life? Where does the power for such action lie?

3. Jesus began his ministry speaking of liberation (Luke 4:18-19). Yet Jesus' first miracle in John's Gospel was at Cana of Galilee where he celebrated a wedding by making wine out of water (John 2:1-11). How did Jesus combine seriousness with joy?

4. A major tension in contemporary Christianity lies between those who assert that liberation is the primary goal of the Christian life, and those who celebrate in the good news of Jesus Christ. Do you know of instances when this tension has been shown? Do you see yourself stressing one position to the exclusion of the other? Which side do you stress? What is the fault with being too serious, or too joyful? Is your Christian community overemphasizing one position?

5. Do the comments you made about self-giving and self-finding help you in wrestling with liberation and celebration? What is the relation of those two sets of themes?

SESSION TWO

BACKGROUND MATERIAL

Chapter Three: *Hurt And Hope;* Chapter Four: *Strength And Vulnerability;* Chapter Five: *Penance And Pardon*

QUESTIONS

1. Read: Matthew   8:16-7   **The Healing Ministry of Jesus**

                              10:1   **Healing by the Disciples**

      Mark   1:32-4a   **The Healing Ministry of Jesus**

      Luke   6:20-3   **Beatitudes for the Hurt**

Hurt is the most universal condition of humanity. We have all been hurt and we have also hurt others. Where is the hurt in your life now? In such times, is it important to be reminded of the hurt which Jesus Christ suffered? (Matthew 27:45-50) How does an understanding of the hurt Jesus Christ suffered help us to reach out beyond our hurt to the hurt of others? Does it help us to offer hope?

2. Read: Matthew   9:35-10:4   **The Power and**

                              10:7-22   **Strength of Jesus and the Disciples**

Matthew 27:11-14   Jesus Christ as the
27:27-31   Suffering King

Strength and vulnerability are the power and restraint of the Christian life. Where and when do you receive strength from God? Where and when do you receive strength from your Christian community? How is your strength shown? Complementing this strength, where and when are you vulnerable to God? Where and when are you vulnerable to others in your community? When are you vulnerable to the world? Are you strong? And are you vulnerable?

3. **Read: Matthew   23:23-8   Woe to the Hypocrites**
     Luke   18:9-14   The Pharisee and the
          Tax-collector
     John   8:3-11   The Adulterous Woman

Ours is an age in which sin is casually asserted and pardon is too easily asked. Is the sense of sin related to the need for grace? When you confess your sins, is it done because you feel separated from God and your neighbor? From where does the power to confess come? When does pardon take place?

4. The medieval acts of *contrition* (recognizing in your heart that you have sinned), *satisfaction* (doing acts of atonement), and *absolution* (being forgiven and told to sin no more) are helpful in remembering the full depth of confession. How might they be used in our day?

SESSION THREE

BACKGROUND MATERIAL

Chapter Six: *Love And Justice;* Chapter Seven: *Commitment And Openness;* Chapter Eight: *Justification And Santification*

QUESTIONS

1. **Read: Micah   6:8   The Demands of God**
   Matthew   22:34-38   The Great Commandment

   Love has often been described as the Christian's relationship with God and one's neighbor; and justice is how one's society seeks fairness for all people. Both love and justice are a part of the Christian whole. How have you participated in your Christian community by being sensitive, forgiving, claiming, and seeking community? How have you participated in society at large to express these same qualities? Examine how you see love seeking justice in one particular social issue (for example, the death penalty).

2. **Read: Acts   9:1-9   Saul's Conversion**

   When did your commitment to Christ begin? Of what did it consist? What did you believe was unalterable? Has this belief changed? Is your level of commitment stronger, weaker, or the same? What is your present commitment to Jesus Christ? In what areas of commitment are you still open to possibilities? In what areas are you already closed?

3. Read: Romans   5:1-2   Justification by Grace Through Faith

Justification and sanctification are often misunderstood, yet they are central parts of every Christian life. At which point in your life were you justified: baptism, an altar call, or a born-again experience? What was your role in that act? What was God's role? Since that experience has your life been a process of sanctification? Have you drawn closer to God?

Would it ever be possible to fall completely away from God? Is the search for Christian wholeness to be understood as the movement from justification to sanctification? How are the complementary terms used throughout **Christian Wholeness** related to sanctification?

SESSION FOUR

BACKGROUND MATERIAL

Chapter Nine: *Speaking And Listening;* Chapter
Ten: *Mediation and Contemplation*

QUESTIONS
1. Read:Matthew 15:21-28 Jesus and the Canaanite Woman

Speaking and listening are essential in the relationship of God with persons. Such a dialogue between
God and humanity is seen most clearly in Jesus
Christ. How do you remember Jesus speaking and
listening to his followers? Is this a part of your
prayer life?

2. Read: Matthew 6:9-15 The Lord's Prayer

In prayer, one may go to one of two extremes—
either by only speaking or only listening. How do
you relate to God in prayer: through speaking, listening, or both?

3. Conversation with God involves both speaking
and listening. How can conversation with God serve
as a model of your relationships with other people?

What is the value of speaking? What is the value of listening?

4. Read: Matthew 26:36-45   Jesus at Gethsemane

Meditation, "doing with God," is the conscious yet nonvocal communication which you may have with God. Have you ever had such prayer? Upon what did you focus: a specific problem, a plea for guidance, or something else? Was there a pulling together of your thoughts with God's thoughts? How might you be more meditative in your prayers?

5. Read: Luke   3:21-22   The Calling of Jesus

Contemplation, "being with God," is the unconscious, receptive, and nonvocal communication which you may have with God. Have you ever had such prayer? Where and when did it happen? How do you describe God's presence with you at such times? How might you become more contemplative in your prayers?

SESSION FIVE

BACKGROUND MATERIAL

Chapter Eleven: *Excellence And Humility;* Chapter
Twelve: *Boredom And Beatitude*

QUESTIONS

1. Read: Matthew   21:1-11   Jesus Entering Jerusalem
**   27:33-37   The Crucifixion**

Excellence and humility are seen together most
clearly in the life of Jesus the Christ. Jesus Christ
serves as our model. How has your life revealed
excellence? How has your life revealed humility?

2. Read: Romans   1:19-23   God in the World

Does our failure to see God in the world create
boredom? Have you experienced boredom? What
was it like? How might one move from boredom to
meaning? Can you recommend the movement from
exhausted living to happiness in Christ to one who is
serenely secular?

3. Read: Luke   11:42-53   Woe to the Pharisees
**   Romans   5:12-14   All Are Sinful**

Boredom seems to be a particular affliction of
those who have many material things. Can boredom

also be experienced by those who have little or no material possessions? Does boredom issue from one's social status or from something deeper? Is boredom just another word for the incompleteness of one's humanity? How can you move from incompleteness to wholeness?

SESSION SIX

BACKGROUND MATERIAL

Chapter Thirteen: *Death And Resurrection*

QUESTIONS

1. Read: Romans   5:12-21   Adam and Christ

Do you believe that death is an ending or a transition?

2. How have you dealt with the death of persons close to you? How have you dealt with the death of millions of persons unknown? How have you prepared for your own death?

3. Someone once said, "The only time you must believe in the resurrection is when one whom you love dies." Is this true, or is the belief of resurrection something we can or must affirm daily despite its seeming impossibility?

4. Have you begun to experience new life in Christ? How does this speak to your own death? How can this free you to serve others?

CONCLUSION

"So the search for Christian wholeness is a finding and a new questioning; it is not possession but being possessed; it knows temptation and failure, but it also knows grace and new beginning."

ABOUT THE AUTHOR

Thomas A. Langford received the A.B. degree from Davidson College, the B.D. degree from Duke Divinity School. and the Ph.D. degree from Duke University.

His teaching experiences have been varied. Early in his career he served as professor of religion in the department of religion, Duke University. Presently, he serves as Dean of the Divinity School. Duke University, as well as professor of systematic theology.

Dean Langford is a frequent speaker on college and university campuses, seminary campuses, retreat centers. He has written many articles and books for publication in the areas of theology and philosophy.

Dean Langford has served the United Methodist Church through participation at Jurisdictional Conferences, the World Methodist Council, and the Division of Ordained Ministry, Board of Higher Education. He is a member of the Western North Carilina Annual Conference.